The Politics of Irish Dissent, 1650–1800

In the same series:

The Irish Dissenting Tradition, 1650–1750
The Religion of Irish Dissent, 1650–1800

The Politics of
Irish Dissent
1650–1800

EDITED BY

Kevin Herlihy

FOUR COURTS PRESS

Set in 10.5 on 12.5 point Ehrhardt for
FOUR COURTS PRESS LTD
55 Prussia Street, Dublin 7, Ireland
E-mail fcp@indigo.ie
and in North America
FOUR COURTS PRESS LTD
c/o ISBS, 5804 NE Hassalo Street, Portland, OR 97213

A catalogue record for this title
is available from the British Library

ISBN 1-85182-301-8 hbk
1-85182-302-6 pbk

Printed in Great Britain
by Antony Rowe Ltd, Chippenham, Wilts.

Contents

Preface

This book is part of a continuing series on the subject of Protestant dissent in Ireland and based on papers originally presented at the third annual conference held at Marsh's Library in Dublin. The current volume is divided into four parts. Part one deals with an historical interpretation of Irish history in regard to dissent and governmental authority in the eighteenth century. In part two there are four chapters addressing various aspects of the political relationship of dissenters to legal statute and different governmental administrations in Ireland. The third part looks at John Wesley's political attitudes. The last part provides a select document relevant to this study.

In the first chapter Dr T.C. Barnard surveys, in an interpretative essay, the crenellation of attitudes and ideas held by those in political authority. His work vividly illustrates the various and changing notions, along with the opinions and perceptions of the political elite during the period of the Sacramental Test Act in eighteenth-century Ireland. The essay shows the tensions and contradictions of thought of those in authority due to the incongruity of the law and the practicalities of life.

The first essay in part two, by Dr Jacqueline Hill, investigates dissenter participation in local politics on the board of alderman, the upper house of Dublin corporation, from 1660 to 1800. Her analysis shows that caution must be taken when evaluating political attitudes; religious affiliation did not necessarily have a direct correspondence to political position or alignment in eighteenth-century Dublin politics. The next chapter, by James McGuire, concentrates on the politically and economically uncertain years immediately after the restoration of Charles II. His essay evaluates James Butler, first duke of Ormond, in relation to his supposed 'natural inclination' of toleration toward Protestant dissenters. This chapter re-evaluates the received doctrine of historians of Ormond on this important issue in Restoration politics. The next two chapters deal with the Sacramental Test which was imposed in 1704 and repealed in 1780. Dr David Hayton begins by looking at how and why the Test came to be. His essay richly provides new information and insights on the politicking, both nationally and locally that surrounded attempts in the political arena of early eighteenth-century Ireland to remove the Test. Next, Dr James Kelly guides us through the intricate and tangled political maneuvers in both Dublin and London in the late 1770s which finally did end the Sacramental Test.

In the next section Revd Robin Roddie surveys some of John Wesley's political attitudes in Ireland. Based on Wesley's reluctance to engage in politics, the chapter investigates his political inclinations in relation to some of the social issues he faced in late eighteenth-century Ireland.

In the last part Dr Raymond Gillespie provides an introduction and reproduction of a poem that depicts the political tension in Dublin between dissenters and the authority of the established church. The poem was most likely written by Joseph Boyse, the pastor of the Wood Street congregation. The poem reveals many of the basic problems that existed between those who believed in the concept of established religion and those who believed in religion based on voluntary participation.

* * *

I would like to express my thanks and appreciation to the people and institutions for their invaluable help in making both the conference and the publication of the proceedings possible. First, to Trinity College, Dublin, for a multitude of assistance in both the running of the conference and the publication of the proceedings; the Department of Modern History at Trinity has been very supportive, and especially Professor Aidan Clarke; the Department of Computer Science at Trinity has not only been helpful and patient in dealing with unexpected problems in this publication, but the preceding ones as well; the Provost and trustees of the Grace Lawless Lee Fund for financial support. I would like to thank Muriel McCarthy for her generosity and care that has made the venue for the papers presented at Marsh's Library such an untroubled event. Many thanks to Four Courts Press for the reception at the library after the day-time papers. I would also like to express my appreciation to the contributors for their work in presenting and publishing their essays. Finally, many thanks must go to those people who have supported the conference by their attendance.

The Government and Irish Dissent, 1704–1780

TOBY C. BARNARD

In 1739, a powerful merchant in Derry revealed that it was essential to remove a papist from a gunner's place in the city. He hoped that the Catholic would be replaced by 'an honest Presbyterian Protestant'. The anxiety arose from one of those rumours of foreign danger which regularly disturbed the ports of eighteenth-century Ireland; also from the fact that the job 'is a gunpowder post', for which 'we may want honest men'. The willingness to entrust this sensitive office to a Presbyterian already well-known in Derry as a teacher reflects how much sectarian tensions within the local Protestant populations had relaxed, certainly since the 1670s and even from the 1690s. Furthermore, the episode suggests that the benefits of the Protestant Ascendancy extended beyond the obvious perquisites of places in parliament and corporations to the seemingly minor offices of the military and civil establishments. Not only was the Presbyterian substitute able to pay the £30 for the gunner's place, he could also gratify the clerk who drew up the commission with the customary couple of guineas.[1] More importantly, the prospective employment uncovered local realities in the distribution of and access to power rather different from those which, since the Test Act of 1704, might have been expected to prevail throughout Ireland. A notion of the Protestant Interest which encompassed dissenters as well as conformists meant that the exclusions promised by the Test were not always realised.

How the Test operated, the variations from place to place and over time, and the extent to which through devices such as the successive Indemnity Acts it was evaded, remain subjects of speculation rather than precise analysis.[2] Only recently has David Hayton in his important study shown the impact of the Test on four of the biggest municipalities in Ulster: Belfast, Derry, Carrickfergus and Coleraine.[3] Even within these boroughs, the timing and severity of the purges

1 Public Record Office of Northern Ireland [hereafter PRONI], D 1649/ 12/51.
2 J.C.Beckett, *Protestant dissent in Ireland 1687–1780* (London, 1948); S.J. Connolly, *Religion, law and power: the making of Protestant Ireland 1660–1760* (Oxford, 1992), pp 160–71; I. McBride, 'Presbyterians in the Penal Era', *Bullán* (1994), I, no. 2, pp. 2–23.
3 D.W. Hayton, 'Exclusion and conformity: the impact of the Sacramental Test on Irish dissenting politics', below, pp. 52–73; cf. L. Clarkson, 'Armagh 1770: portrait of an urban community', in D. Harkness and M. O'Dowd (eds.), *The town in Ireland: Historical Studies XIII* (Belfast, 1981), p. 84.

of Protestant nonconformists differed. Otherwise, because we are still ignorant of patterns of local office-holding, whether in corporations, the magistracy, the customs and revenue or the military, the seriousness of the purges announced by the Test of 1704, and the reality of what did occur, continue to excite divergent views. In these, modern commentators merely echo the disagreements of their eighteenth-century predecessors. Of the latter, some contended that the Test was strictly applied and denied the Protestant state in Ireland the services of many useful members; others believed that few of substance and loyalty were thereby excluded. Unfortunately, even when we have lists of the personnel who ran Irish towns and counties, it is unlikely that great precision will be possible about confessional affiliations. Dangerous inferences may continue to be drawn from the evidence of names and supposed ethnic origin as to denomination.

In default of any comprehensive studies of the local effects of the Test, other than the pioneering enquiry of Dr Hayton, it may be appropriate to look again at one or two of the obvious questions raised by the existence of the Test between 1704 and 1780. Although the precise manner in which the Test was introduced into Ireland, together with the initiative behind it (among English and Irish churchmen and politicians), have never been definitively established, the origins of the measure are more readily understood than its long continuance.[4] Despite its being imposed on Ireland almost by sleight of hand, and its hitting—supposedly fortuitously—Protestant dissenters as well as Catholics, each of the attempts to have the Test repealed failed. Indeed, by 1733, enthusiasm among the gentry who sat in the Dublin parliament for repeal had so far dwindled that thereafter the attempt was abandoned for more than a generation.

Just as the motives behind and daily operations of the penal laws against Catholics have been re-examined, a similar reconsideration of how those same laws touched the lives of dissenters would be timely. In essence, the measures against Irish Catholics have been likened to the disabilities laid on Catholics in Britain and on religious dissidents in confessional states throughout Europe. These comparisons, however, show the peculiarity of the Irish situation, where, uniquely, a majority of the inhabitants faced penalties. As to why these restrictions were laid on Irish Catholics, if the reality of fears that they might again take up arms to recover lands, places and power is acknowledged, greater stress has lately been placed on the religious impulse. Protestants in Ireland hoped that, were the right conditions to be created, the Catholics could be converted. Others have shown that Irish Protestants, never united over either the justice or efficacy of legal severity, soon connived at the increasingly public practice of

4   J.G. Simms, 'The making of a penal law (2 Anne, c. 6), 1703–4', in Simms, *War and politics in Ireland, 1649–1730*, edited by D.W. Hayton and G. O'Brien (London and Ronceverte, 1986), 263–76. Also, Connolly, *Religion, law and power*, pp. 272–3; D.W. Hayton, 'Ireland and the English ministers, 1707–1716' D. Phil. dissertation, Oxford University (1975), pp. 30–41.

popery. In this situation, with few of the laws stringently applied, Protestants wrangled over whether it was wise to retain them on the statute book so that when an emergency arose they could be activated, or whether it would be better to allow Catholics a formal toleration at least of their faith.[5] The gap between nominal ferocity and the prevalent forbearance throughout much of eighteenth-century Ireland has been variously interpreted. For many the inability of the Protestant state in Ireland to implement the penal laws could be taken as evidence of its feebleness and lethargy. Artificially created and artificially maintained, it attracted the active support of only 10 per cent of the island's inhabitants. Others accused the authors and supporters of the penalties of hypocrisy, as they screened a concern to keep estates and offices behind protestations of religious zealotry. Then, too, there is a view that soon enough the penal laws were emptied of any vitality and were instead turned into showy carapaces, calculated to intimidate but not to work. Above all, perhaps, although the Catholic priests and property owners were massively inconvenienced by aspects of the laws, even their erratic enforcement did not inhibit the steady improvement in the condition of the Irish Catholic Church.[6]

Much the same might be said about the fortunes of Irish dissent, or at least its most vigorous manifestations of Ulster Presbyterianism, the Quakers and—from the 1740s—the Methodists. The collapse of some of the older sects which had emerged during the anarchic 1650s, such as the Independents or Congregationalists and Baptists, while affected by the incentives to conform contained with the laws, nevertheless owed more to genetic attrition. So far as the Presbyterians and Quakers were concerned, social, economic and legal pressures had pushed aristocratic and gentry members into the established Church

5   For the varying interpretations of the thinking behind and effects of the laws, see: T.C. Barnard, 'Protestants and the Irish language, 1675–1725', *Journal of Ecclesiastical History* (1993), xliv, 243–72; Connolly, *Religion, law and power*, pp. 307–13; S.J. Connolly, 'Reformers and high-flyers: the post-revolution Church' in A. Ford, J. McGuire and K. Milne (eds.), *As by law established: the Church of Ireland since the Reformation* (Dublin, 1995), pp. 152–65; Hayton, 'Ireland and the English ministers', pp. 18–29; Hayton, 'Did Protestantism fail in early eighteenth-century Ireland? Charity schools and the enterprise of religious and social reformation, c. 1690–1730', in Ford, et al., *As by law established*, pp. 166–86; Hayton, 'The high church party in the Irish convocation 1703–1713', forthcoming; C.D.A. Leighton, *Catholicism in a Protestant kingdom: a study of the Irish 'ancien regime'* (London, 1994).
6   The most comprehensive recent assessment of the fortunes of Catholicism is T.P. Power and K. Whelan (eds.), *Endurance and emergence: Catholics in Ireland in the eighteenth century* (Dublin, 1990). For local studies: J. Kelly, 'The Catholic Church in the diocese of Ardagh, 1650–1870', in R. Gillespie and G. Moran (eds.), *Longford: essays in county history* (Dublin, 1991), pp. 63–91; F. Ó Fearghail, 'The Catholic Church in county Kilkenny, 1600–1800' in W. Nolan and K. Whelan (eds.), *Kilkenny: history and society* (Dublin, 1990), pp. 197–249.

of Ireland by the early eighteenth century.[7] Not all cut their links with the dissenting congregations. Occasional conformity may have been practised, so as to
qualify the ambitious for the offices essential to their status and economic well-
being. When in Dublin, it may have been easier to keep up connections with the
non-conformist churches than in the countryside where such congregations
were sparse. The Wills family, for example, squires who settled themselves in
the Roscommon countryside, had for two generations participated in the running of the Dublin Presbyterian church in Strand Street.[8] In addition to gentlemen who continued to sympathise through sentiment, family tradition and conviction with dissenting kinsfolk and acquaintances, the hold of Presbyterianism
among educated townspeople and reports from the north of Ireland which heart-
ened the champions of episcopacy, neither the fierce doctrinal controversies of
the 1720s nor the dramatic exodus of Ulster Scots to the New World dimin-
ished the size and vigour of the nonconformist population.[9]

Often observers relied on impressions rather than meticulous enquiries to
gauge the scale of the problem. Unlike the Catholics who were counted across
the country in 1731–33, only the occasional local survey revealed the numbers
of dissenters. During the 1720s, in at least two Dublin parishes, the dissenters
were totted up. Reassuringly they amounted to fewer than one-sixth or one-
eighth of the strength of the conformists.[10] Similarly in the 1730s, bishops noted
in their visitations sizeable concentrations of Protestant dissenters, but only in
single parishes within their dioceses: Seapatrick in Dromore and Lifford in
Derry.[11] By the 1750s and 1760s, other accounts attested to the prevalence of
dissenters within towns such as Armagh, Belfast, Downpatrick and Monaghan.
Numbers or proportions are suspiciously round, thus provoking scepticism about
the processes through which they had been found if not about the situation
which they reveal.[12]

The lack of any national censuses to ascertain totals of dissenters, and indeed the habit of lumping nonconformists and conformists together as 'Protes-

7   T.C. Barnard, 'Identities, ethnicity and tradition among Irish dissenters, c. 1650–1750'
    in K. Herlihy (ed.), *The Irish dissenting tradition 1650–1750* (Dublin, 1995), pp. 34–5.
8   Notes by G.T.B. Clements from Wood Street and Strand Street congregations, 5 Febru-
    ary 1730 [1], 12 August 1731, 25 March 1738, Presbyterian Historical Society, Belfast,
    MS CR 437/B; National Library of Ireland [herafter NLI], MS 3203; M.L. Legg (ed.),
    *The Synge Letters: Bishop Edward Synge to his daughter, Alicia, Roscommon to Dublin,
    1746–1752* (Dublin, 1996), p. xliv.
9   The present histories of Presbyterianism in the eighteenth century, J.S. Reid, *History of
    the Presbyterian Church in Ireland*, W.D. Killen (ed.) (3 vols, Belfast, 1867); and P. Brooke,
    Ulster Presbyterianism: the historical perspective 1610–1970 (Belfast, 1994), will soon be
    amplified in Ian McBride, *Scripture politics* (forthcoming).
10 Pearse Street Public Library, Dublin, Gilbert MS 35, p. 389; Representative Church
    Body, Dublin [hereafter RCB], MS P. 276/12/1, p. 104.
11 RCB, MS GS 2/7/3/34 (Dromore), p. 6; ibid., (Derry), p. 11.
12 Pearse Street Library, Gilbert MS 36, pp. 373–5, 378, 388.

tants', may reasonably be taken as a sign that Protestant dissent excited fewer fears than Catholicism.[13] Moreover, for those who persisted in the venerable tradition of urging Protestant unity in the face of Irish Catholic strength, the Protestant Interest necessarily comprehended all who accepted the basics of doctrine. In this spirit the disunity exposed and exacerbated by the Test Act— at best a regrettable necessity, at worst a potentially fatal political miscalcula- tion—should be corrected by the practical toleration allowed the peaceable and orthodox. Impressionism rather than exactitude in estimating nonconformist numbers may speak of indifference on the part of the Church of Ireland au- thorities. Even so what the figures conveyed could disquiet. In 1760, for exam- ple, the 12,000 inhabitants of Belfast, apart from 500 papists, were divided be- tween two-thirds or three-quarters dissenters and the small remnant conform- ists. In 1763, the town of Monaghan was thought to contain two hundred houses. Half the townspeople were described as Catholics; two-thirds of the remainder were again Presbyterians. In Downpatrick, a different situation prevailed, with its 450 houses split equally between Catholics, Church of Ireland and dissent- ers.[14] In Armagh city, the proportions differed: 191 papist families, 166 of the Church of Ireland and 110 dissenters.[15] Often notions of the dissenters' strength, like that of the Catholics, were conveyed by their chapels. The building of meeting houses had earlier signalled the penetration of Presbyterians into new districts, such as Drogheda and Sligo. In Belfast by 1763, the preponderance of the Pres- byterians was illustrated by their three meeting houses, along with a fourth used by 'some fanatic sect'. The Church of Ireland possessed only one building for worship. By contrast, the weakness of Protestant dissent throughout such of the south of Ireland was exemplified by Wexford town where there was no meet- ing house recorded in 1761. Yet this was not invariably the case of Munster and Leinster.[16] Waterford, by contrast, in 1758 was thought to have two Church of Ireland churches, separate meeting houses for Presbyterians, Baptists and Quakers, as well as two mass houses.[17]

The physical presence of buildings dedicated to worship according to alter- native rites embodied the problems of Catholicism and Protestant dissent in eighteenth-century Ireland, which so far from abating seemed on this evidence to be growing. The buildings themselves uncovered more of the ambiguities in

13 National Archive [hereafter NA], Dublin, M 2466; *An abstract of the number of Protes- tants and Popish families in the several counties and provinces of Ireland* (Dublin, 1736); T.P. Cunningham, 'The 1766 religious census, Kilmore and Ardagh', *Breifne* (1961), i, no. 4, pp. 358, 360.
14 Pearse Street Library, Gilbert MS 36, pp. 373, 378, 388; R. Pococke, *Irish Tours*, J McVeigh (ed.) (Dublin, 1995), p. 38.
15 Pearse Street Library, Gilbert MS 36, p. 378; Clarkson, 'Armagh 1770', p. 84.
16 Ibid., p. 374.
17 Ibid., p. 373; J. Walton, 'The earliest Presbyterian register of Waterford', *Irish Ancestor* (1981), xiii, pp. 94–8.

official attitudes. In general, we must suppose that staunch conformists did not venture into these strange structures. Just as the fabrics and furnishings of the Church of Ireland tabernacles improved, so the same changing expectations of comfort and convenience transformed the interiors of at least urban Catholic chapels and dissenters' meeting houses.[18] Yet, for all their enhanced allure, most responsible for the making and enforcement of the laws had only the haziest concept of what went on inside. But, while these buildings might remind uncomfortably of the Anglican failure to bring the recalcitrant to heel, churches could attract support from across the denominational boundaries. When in the 1720s the new organ at St. Michan's parish church in Dublin received subscriptions' from a Catholic priest and a dissenting teacher, they may have been displaying a sense of local solidarity with their quarter and its amenities.[19] Equally, they may have paid in order to buy off awkward enquiries into their own activities. More surprising, perhaps, was the willingness of adherents of the established Church to assist financially with the construction of meeting houses for dissenters. Donations might be made from sentiment, as conformists remembered the sects in which their forbears had originated.[20] In Ulster, and the borderlands into which the Ulster Scots were gravitating by the early eighteenth century, landowners keen to promote new settlement by the industrious and skilled appreciated the magnetism of purpose-built places of worship. First at such places as Killyleagh, Creggan, and Monaghan, help of this sort was given.[21] However, as the craze for promoting the linen manufacture caught hold of more proprietors, so the necessity of assisting in the erection of dissenting meeting houses was understood. As the town of Sligo was drawn into the orbit of Ulster linen, one local landlord leased the land for a meeting house at a low rent while a second gave £10 towards the costs.[22] Ten years earlier each had helped towards the enlargement and modernisation of the Church of Ireland building.[23] Now, as the agent of one candidly told his

18 NLI, MS 2714, p. 121; S. ffeary-Smyrl, 'Theatres of Worship: dissenting meeting houses in Dublin 1650–1750' in Herlihy, *Irish dissenting tradition*, pp. 49–64; St Patrick's College, Maynooth, *Ecclesiastical art of the penal era* (Maynooth, 1995). See, too, the artefacts in the collections of the Presbyterian Historical Society in Belfast.

19 E.J. Young, 'Eighteenth-century documents relating to the parish of St Michan, Dublin', Journal of the Royal Society of Antiquaries of Ireland (1933), lxiii, p. 119.

20 NLI, MS 409.

21 PRONI, D 1759/1D/10, pp. 157–8; J. Donaldson, *A historical and statistical account of the barony of Upper Fews in the County of Armagh, 1838* (Dundalk, 1923), pp. 11–12; *Records of the General Synod of Ulster 1691–1820* (3 vols, Belfast, 1870), I , pp. 443, 476.

22 NLI, MS 5830, p. 81; Southampton University LIbrary, Broadlands MSS, BR 142/1/11.

23 Ibid., BR 2/7; NA, M 2533, p. 366; C. Tyndall, *The ancient parish and church of St John the Baptist, Sligo* (Dublin, 1962), p. 18.

employer, £10 would prove a good investment, since 'it will bring up many people from the north, which makes the lots in the town and the lands at a distance give a much better price'.[24]

These often imprecise enumerations of dissenters, coupled with the striking enthusiasm for them as tenants and workers, uncover the disparity between the theoretical severity and daily freedom. Thus, while frontal attacks on the laws had failed to have them repealed, they might simply wither away through desuetude. Why this did not happen, with the laws maintained until 1780 and perhaps as many as half its potential beneficiaries legally excluded from the favours of the Protestant Ascendancy, requires more explanation.

II

Objective evidence about the size and nature of the dissenting population might be hard to assemble. It was not missing. Notwithstanding the absence of any comprehensive national surveys, enquiries were made, particularly in Ulster, in order to quantify some aspects of the problem. In the 1720s, for instance, the authorities interested themselves in cataloguing the leading landowners in the north. The resulting lists, for all their omissions and inaccuracies, cheered those who had argued consistently that few of any consequence in landed society had been disabled from local service by the Test. Moreover, the pressure added by the Test to the others already encouraging a nominal conformity seemed to be clear in the recorded defectors from the faith of their fathers.[25] Similar interest was taken in the local militia and the extent to which it had been enfeebled either by the temporary inclusion of nonconformists during the emergency of 1715 or by their exclusion at other times.[26] The record of who was or was not debarred by the Test from local office, or how dissenters behaved when entrusted with responsibilities, tended to support preconceived notions about Protestant dissent as either dangerous or harmless. Frequently these notions derived less from close scrutiny of the current scene than from inherited prejudices. Historians have been too ready to assume, perhaps, that the tenacious anti-Catholic and anti-Presbyterian feelings which persisted in Hanoverian Ireland (as in contemporary England) were rooted in material worries and rational apprehensions. Such did, of course, exist. Nevertheless, the role of an irrational atavism needs to be considered.

24 Southampton University Library, BR 142/1/11.
25 Lambeth Palace Library, MS 1742, ff.49–56; Royal Irish Academy, Dublin, MS 24 K 19.
26 Christ Church, Oxford, Wake MS 12, ff.145, 147, 323, 370; 13, ff.66–7; PRONI, D 2092/1/3, 30.

As the combatants girded themselves for battle over the Test yet again in
1733, scurrilous allegations abounded. One otherwise unmemorable piece of
doggerel printed in Dublin at the time adverted to the 'past conduct of Jack
Presbyter Blue', who 'tumbled crown and mitre', murdering the king, Wentworth
and Laud.[27] The prevalence of such readings of history obliged the dissenters to
vindicate themselves. Too often they were misrepresented 'as a turbulent faction that have been engaged for one hundred and eighty years in one uninter-
rupted course of rebellion and disloyalty'.[28] These hostile characterisations were
not easily effaced. In part, the historical interpretations of the seventeenth century which blamed Presbyterian malcontents for lighting the fuse which ig-
nited first the Bishops' War in Scotland, next the English civil wars and the
regicide of 1649, not to mention the broils over Exclusion between 1678 and
1681, was too popular (most authoritatively in Clarendon's *History*) to be dis-
carded. It rested too on a widely held suspicion that Presbyterians and papists
were joined in a devilish anti-Christian pact. Few pieces of concrete evidence
from Ireland's recent past indicated such a conspiracy. Yet the underlying simi-
larity of Presbyterian and Catholic attitudes toward civil authority, the willingness of each to obey a superior spiritual power, and so a propensity to rebel and
depose or kill the ungodly ruler, gave greater credibility to the Anglicans who
urged vigilance against both adversaries.[29]

In Ireland, those red-letter days of the Anglican calendar lifted from England, notably the anniversaries of Charles I's execution and Charles II's restoration, kept alive remembrance of what papists and dissenters had done. Other
celebrations peculiar to Ireland, such as the discovery of the plot of 1641, the
arrival of William III, the relief of Derry and the victory at the Boyne, so far
from stressing the shared suffering and common heroism of Ulster Scots and
English Protestant settlers, could perpetuate rivalries and animosities.[30] Even
more recent occasions when Presbyterians had vied with their conformist neighbours to display their loyalty could worsen resentments. 1715, no less than 1688–

---

27 *A new ballad supposed to be wrote by a Reverend D-n in the North* ([Dublin], 1733).
28 *A vindication of Protestant dissenters* (Dublin, [1733]), p. 4.
29 D. Ashe, *A sermon preach'd before the honourable House of Commons ... January the 31st,
    1703/4* (Dublin, 1704), pp. 10–11; St George Ashe, *A sermon preach'd at Christ's Church
    in Dublin, January the 30th 1715/16* (Dublin, 1715/16), pp. 8, 14; P. Delany, *A sermon
    preach'd in Christ-Church Dublin ... January 30, 1737* (Dublin, 1737[8]), pp. 18–20; J
    Echlin, *The royal martyr* (Dublin, 1713), pp. 8–13, 20–3; J. Lawson, *A sermon preached
    ... the 23rd of October, 1753* (Dublin, 1753), pp. 12–13; M. Philips, *A sermon preached ...
    the 23rd October, 1745* (Dublin 1745), pp. 15–16; J. Swift, 'A sermon on the martyrdom
    of K. Charles I' in Swift, *Irish tracts 1720–1723 and sermons*, H. Davis and L. Landa
    (eds) (Oxford 1948, reprinted 1968), pp. 220–8; W. Tisdall, *A sample of true-blew Presby-
    terian loyalty* (Dublin, 1709); Tisdall, *The conduct of the dissenters in Ireland* (Dublin,
    1715); Tisdall, *The Case of the Sacramental Test, Stated and Argued* (Dublin, 1715).
30 T.C. Barnard, 'The uses of 23 October 1641 and Irish Protestant celebrations' *English
    Historical Review* (1991), cvi, pp. 911–20.

90 or the 1640s, was a moment when the ricketty Protestant state in Ireland welcomed the help of all who were prepared to rally to its defence. The ban on Presbyterians serving in the militia was relaxed temporarily, but the Irish Parliament balked at any permanent abandonment of the Test. The results of admitting Presbyterians into the militias in counties Down and Antrim were not always happy. The sudden enthusiasm for Presbyterian loyalists came quick on the heels of the Tory reaction of 1710–14. Then the Presbyterians had been harried, state aid had been withdrawn and instead the legal penalties had been applied. Now in 1715, Presbyterians entrusted with arms and authority, sometimes used them to avenge themselves on their tormentors. Prominent churchmen, vexed by rough searches of their property and by allegations of Jacobite sympathies, acquired fresh reasons to hate the local Presbyterians.[31] The assertiveness, even aggression, with which Presbyterians exploited the powers temporarily allowed them by the state, may have turned contemporaries against any permanent change. The ability of the Presbyterian Church, with its kirk sessions, synods and assemblies, to create an autonomous institution through which much of the detail of its adherents' daily lives was regulated, warned of what Presbyterians might accomplish if they were able to colonise the magistracy and militia. Already, before their rule was ended by the Test Act, the corporations of Belfast and Derry had fallen to their control.[32] But the more that official generosity was withheld from the Presbyterians, the more they were obliged to retreat into their own redoubts, strengthening the worry that what they aspired to and were in the process of creating was a state within the state. Again, the parallels with anxieties about the Catholics, who, despite their seeming peaceableness, held fast to secret loyalties and beliefs alien to those of British and Irish Protestants, were strong. And, as with the Catholics, although Protestants enjoyed amicable relationships with dissenters, many distinguished between individuals, innocuous enough, and nonconformists and papists in the abstract and aggregate, who were to be feared and repressed. Also, the less that was known of what occurred in the meeting houses and kirk sessions, the more imaginations conjured the sinister.

In short, then, upholders of the Test appealed to the real and the imagined. In the case of the Ulster Presbyterians, the two elements were fused in such a way as to strengthen hostility. At first sight such an argument may look willfully perverse. Many of the developments mentioned already—such as the loss of powerful supporters, emigration to North America, greater appreciation of the work ethic associated with the Presbyterians—suggest a weakening of animosi-

31 J. Smythe to W. Smythe, 6 February 1714[15], 15 March 1715[16], 14 September 1716, NLI, PC 449; *The report of the judges of assize for the north-east circuit of Ulster* (np, 1716).
32 J. Agnew, *Belfast merchant families in the seventeenth century* (Dublin, 1996), pp. 91–104; Hayton, 'Exclusion and conformity'.

ties. Yet, some of the changes happening in the 1720s supported unfriendly
evaluations of the dissenters. It was difficult certainly to deny the links between
severe weather, bad harvests, heavy mortality of livestock and near famine conditions, and the impulse to remove to America. Because some sufferers complained that what made their lot intolerable were the extra burdens imposed by
rapacious landlords and Anglican clergy greedy for their tithes, members of the
established church viewed the plight of Ulster less kindly. Defenders of the
official social and ecclesiastical order turned an allegation often made against
the impoverished Irish Catholics against the Ulster Scots Presbyterians: want
of industry explained their predicament. At the same time, others attributed
their restiveness to their subversive political and theological principles. The
'richer sort' who planned to emigrate did so because they averred that 'if they
stay in Ireland their children will be slaves'. Meanwhile their preachers exploited the prophetic and providential modes, telling their auditors that 'God
had appointed a country to them to dwell in (naming New England) and desires
them to depart'. The utopia of a new world was invoked. Letters from New
England were said to depict it as free from taxes, and 'that all men are there
upon a level and that it is a good poor man's country'. Reports of such views
circulating and inspiring the exodus reinforced a view of the Ulster Scots as
alienated from the institutions and values of the Protestant state in Ireland.[33]

Concurrent with the economic distress which drove many Presbyterians from
Ireland was a rift in the Presbyterian ranks. The effects of these acrimonious
and very public wrangles, ostensibly over whether or not to subscribe to the
Westminster Confession, ought to have pleased champions of the Church of
Ireland.[34] But, whatever short-term disruption resulted, the grip of the Presbyterians over much of Ulster was not loosened. The secession of the 'new light'
ministers into a separate organisation, the Synod of Antrim, gave greater coher-
ence to a group whose reasonable approach to the controverted issues of belief
chimed well with the tolerant within the Church of Ireland.[35] Common as-
sumptions, notably the inability of human reason to reach certain answers about
the fundamentals of Christianity and therefore the absurdity of compelling all
to accept particular doctrines and practices as essential to salvation, led to a
shared wish that consciences should not be forced by insisting on sacramental
qualifications as prerequisites for holding office. Such views could not prevail

---

33 PRONI, D 2092/1/3, 309; Ibid., D 2860/11/28, 31, 33; Trinity College Dublin [here-
    after TCD], MS 3974/9.
34 Christ Church, Wake MS 13, ff 150, 155.
35 I. McBride, 'The school of virtue: Francis Hutcheson, Irish Presbyterians and the Scot-
    tish Enlightenment' in R. Eccleshall, V. Geoghegan and D.G. Boyce (eds.), *Political thought
    in Ireland since the seventeenth century* (London, 1993), pp. 73–99; M.A. Stewart, 'Ra-
    tional dissent in eighteenth-century Ireland', in K. Haakonssen (ed.), *Enlightenment and
    religion: rational dissent in eighteenth-century Britain* (Cambridge, 1996), pp. 43–59.

over those who insisted on maintaining the Test Act. The 'new light' shone more brightly among the educated and urban, encouraging them to adopt and promote higher standards of urbanity and civility. It united Presbyterian exponents and exemplars of politeness with the like-minded within the Anglican community.[36] Unhappily, it also turned these Presbyterians, with their strident insistence on ethical and cultural superiority, into competitors, both against their more numerous traditionalist brethren who had stayed within the Synod of Ulster and against the elegant clergy and laity of the Church of Ireland. The Presbyterian clergy, thanks to its well-developed connections with the Scottish universities (notably Glasgow) and the Low Countries, was refreshed at the wells of pure enlightenment. Yet, there were sources other than the lectures and books of Francis Hutcheson from which civic responsibility and reasonableness could be learnt.

A multiplicity of influences went into the intellectual and cultural formation of the Church of Ireland clergy. Without a full prosopography of these clerics, and more detailed studies of the curriculum and teaching at Trinity College Dublin during the period, we are left to guess the strongest forces. What is clear is the interest of many Church of Ireland dignitaries and incumbents in the philanthropic, material and moral improvements so loudly advocated by Presbyterian writers.[37] Only in a few communities, mainly the towns and villages of Ulster, did the Church of Ireland and Presbyterians compete directly. So it was chiefly in their distinct spheres that these rivals advertised their achievements. On well-run estates, such as Samuel Madden's at Manor Waterhouse, or at the palace and surrounding demesne of successive bishops at Elphin and Cloyne, leaders of the Church of Ireland made good their claims to be in the vanguard.[38] Maybe modern historians have been too ready to accept the claims of the militantly enlightened dissenters, particularly of the 'new light' persuasion, to direct the accelerating movement to reasonableness, politeness,

36 M.A. Stewart, 'John Smith and the Molesworth circle', *Eighteenth-century Ireland* (1987), ii, pp. 89–102.
37 T. Breviter, *A sermon preached in the parish church of Badony ... May 24th 1730* (Dublin, 1730), pp. 9, 20; J. Trail, *A sermon preached at Christ-Church, Dublin, on the 7th of February, 1779* (Dublin, 1779); T.C. Barnard, 'Protestantism, ethnicity and Irish identities, 1660–1760' in A. Claydon and I. McBride (eds.), *Protestantism and national identity* (Cambridge, forthcoming); L.E. Klein, 'Liberty, manners and politeness in early eighteenth-century England', *Historical Journal* (1989) xxxii, pp. 583–605; N.C. Landsman, 'Presbyterians and provincial society: the evangelical Enlightenment in the west of Scotland, 1740–1775', in J. Dwyer and R.B. Sher (eds.), *Sociability and society: eighteenth-century Scotland* (Edinburgh, 1993), pp. 194–206; McBride, 'The school of virtue'; N. Phillipson, 'Politics, politeness and the anglicization of early eighteenth-century Scottish culture', in R.A. Mason (ed.), *Scotland and England 1286–1815* (Edinburgh, 1987), pp. 226–42.
38 NA, M 2533, pp 464–5; T.C. Barnard, 'Improving clergymen, 1660-1760', in Ford, et al., *As by law established*, pp. 136–51; *The Letters of Lord Chief Baron Edward Willes to the Earl of Warwick, 1757–1762* J. Kelly (ed.) (Aberystwyth, 1990), p. 94.

cultivation and 'modernity'. The self-satisfied who established the tone to be
followed by their neighbours in the Ulster towns irritated both those within
their own localities who adhered still to the fundamentals of Scripture and those
of other denominations who had long contested for spiritual and doctrinal superiority. Thus, if the polish and urbanity of the rational Presbyterians brought
them closer in manners and outlook to a minority within the Protestant Ascendancy, it separated them from the conservative majority. In addition, the
avatars of the 'new light', with their willingness to jettison traditional doctrines
and reconsider not just the relationship between churches and the state but also
the nature of the state, revived anxieties about their association with heterodoxy
and republicanism. Try as they might, respectable dissenters could not free
themselves from the taint of heresy and rebelliousness spread by the writings
and teachings of their outspoken members. In fact the variety of opinions which
flourished among Presbyterians within Ireland by the mid-eighteenth century
enabled their doctrines to appeal both to the consciously urbane and the rustic
fundamentalists. As a result, the doctrinal and institutional disunity which might
otherwise have delighted the Church of Ireland merely confirmed the view of
the latter that Presbyterianism still exhibited the attributes of the chameleon.
In the past, and perhaps still, these qualities made it a willing host for the ambitions of the papists, and threatened to destroy the structures of society and
state.[39]

The eagerness of the generous to admit orthodox dissenters into the Irish
Protestant Ascendancy, and to treat them as united in beliefs and interest with
the members of the Church of Ireland, conceals the extent to which traditional
hostility continued and grew throughout the eighteenth century. There remained
objective grounds for worry: the question of numbers, the existence and vitality
of the separate Presbyterian congregations and doctrines. Moreover, separation, if no longer accounted a sin by the supporters of a lax pluralism, had not
lost its ability to divide. Back in the 1670s, a future Church of Ireland bishop
had considered whether or not a Christian might with a safe conscience attend
conventicles. He had answered with a categorical no. Schism was, above all,
sinful. Furthermore, such separation disturbed peace, rejected established authority and ruptured the society 'of which they should be members'.[40] Such
opinions, unfashionable as they seem to those who are seduced by the blandish-
ments of the irenic and inclusive, nevertheless represented a too often overlooked tradition among the upholders of the Church of Ireland Ascendancy.
Although the restatement of such conservative thinking when the privileges of
the Church of Ireland were being dismantled in the 1770s and 1780s is now
taken more seriously as expressing an important, though rebarbative, outlook,

---

39 See the sources cited in note 29.
40 A. Dopping to Capt. Foley, December 1673-March 1674, NLI, PC 515.

its survival throughout the eighteenth century needs to be traced carefully.[41] Those who opposed the Toleration Act in 1719 and the repeated bids to have the Test removed, since they included some of the bishops most conspicuous as defenders of an Irish against an English interest (such as William King of Dublin and Edward Synge of Tuam), have sometimes been seen as inspired by an instinctive anti-English sentiment.[42] The Test Act had originally been copied and introduced from England, and as such was resented as fresh evidence of Ireland's constitutional subordination. Similarly, the vain efforts to have it lifted and to substitute toleration came—in the main—from London, and could be regarded as another instance of the persistent wish to conform Ireland more closely to English norms. Accurately enough those who resisted legal concessions to Irish Catholics and nonconformists could demonstrate that both constituted much larger and more menacing groups than did their counterparts in England.[43] Yet, if something in the unwillingness of the Irish Parliament to abandon the Test was owed to reflexive anti-English feelings, doctrinal traditionalism and perceptions of the danger still posed by Catholics and Presbyterians played greater parts.

In the end, in order to explain the long survival of these discriminatory measures, a blend of justified fears and irrational prejudices needs to be reconstructed. Just as Catholics enjoyed many of the advantages of a practical freedom of worship notwithstanding the continuance of legal disabilities, so too the growth and functioning of Presbyterian churches were scarcely impeded by the law. Dissenters contented themselves with this forbearance, rather than risk new controversy and defeat with a parliamentary campaign. However, more than the arguments of natural justice and equity rendered this situation offensive. So long as statutes survived by which the dissenters could be penalised they were prey to localised campaigns and periodic panics unleashed by vindictive neighbours. Some of these tensions which came into the open in the 1770s and 1790s had long roots which the patient may in time trace in the occasional excitements of the 1740s, 1720s, 1715 and earlier.[44]

Those who had pushed unavailingly in the early eighteenth century for the

---

41 The outlook is evident in, for example, R. Woodward, *The present state of the Church of Ireland* (Dublin, 1787), and Archbishop Agar, on whom we await Peter McDonagh's dissertation. Earlier expressions occur in: J. Smythe to W. Smythe, 6 December 1749, 7 March 1752, NLI, PC 449.

42 Christ Church, Wake MS 13, ff.108, 113, 116–8, 123–4, 128, 132–3; P. McNally, ' "Irish and English interests": national conflict within the Church of Ireland episcopate in the reign of George I', *Irish Historical Studies* (1995), xxix, pp. 295–314; P. O'Regan, 'Archbishop William King (1650–1729) and the constitution of Church and State', PhD dissertation, University College Cork, (2 vols, 1996), ii, pp. 405–61.

43 Christ Church, Wake MS 13, ff.98, 132–4, 145; TCD, MS 750/5/165–7, 171–2, 189.

44 PRONI, T. 1392; *Faulkner's Dublin Journal*, 18–22 October 1743; P.J. Larkin, ' "Popish Riot" in south Co. Derry, 1725', *Seanchas Ard Mhacha* (1975-6), viii, pp. 97–110; *Report of the judges ... for the north-east circuit of Ulster.*

relaxation of the legal penalties took comfort from two interconnected developments in Irish politics. A principal theatre of war between 1689 and 1691 was Ulster. This contrasted with the Cromwellian campaigns of 1649 to 1652, in which the province had hardly featured.[45] The forwardness of Ulstermen, especially from the north-west, created durable links with William III and some of his entourage and earned the rewards of victory. The richest prize on which the winners had set their sights, the vast estate of Lord Antrim, eluded them.[46] However, other estates fell into their laps, together with assorted offices and grants. Among the lucky were inter-related families from Donegal and Londonderry, such as the Cairnes, Conynghams, Lennoxes, Leslies and Nesbitts, into which the opportunist William Conolly married.[47] Through the city of Derry and the interests of the London companies in the region there existed already channels along which the ambitious and enterprising could move from the locality into the expanding worlds of London business and banking.[48] The extent to which this happened, and the degree to which members of the same dynasties also took over the Dublin customs, revenue and government, remain to be established. What can be discerned clearly is the success of these families, with Conolly the most ostentatious. Their new eminence altered the balance within the Irish parliament and administration. Hitherto both had been dominated by the settler and *converso* families of Leinster and Munster. Now the latter had to struggle for supremacy against the greatly afforced Ulster contingents. So, throughout the early eighteenth century, as the balance tilted first towards and then away from the Munster *squadrone* of the Brodricks and the Boyles, the primacy established originally by the leading Munster settlers, the Boyles, earls of Cork and Burlington and Orrery, was challenged.[49]

45 T.C. Barnard, 'New opportunities for British settlement: Ireland 1650–1700', in R. Louis (ed.), *Oxford history of the British Empire* (Oxford, forthcoming), i.

46 Derry corporation minute book 1688–1704, 12 February 1690[1], 15 January 1691[2], PRONI, LA 79/2A/2; ibid., D 1449/12/15,16.

47 G. Kirkham, ' "No more to be got off the cat but the skin": management, landholding and economic change on the Murray of Broughton estate, 1670–1755' in W. Nolan, L. Ronayne and M. Dunlevy (eds.), *Donegal: history and society* (Dublin, 1995), pp. 357–74; H.C. Lawlor, *A history of the family of Cairnes or Cairns* (London, 1906); A. Nesbitt, *History of the family of Nisbet or Nesbitt in Scotland and Ireland* (Torquay, [1898]); P.L. Pielou, *The Leslies of Tarbert, County Kerry, and their forbears* (Dublin, 1935); A.I. Young, *300 years of Inishowen* (Belfast, 1929).

48 G. Nesbitt to J. Bonnell, 29 May 1717, NLI, PC 435; PRONI, D 1449/12/15; Lawlor, *Family of Cairnes*, pp. 82–6, 144, 168–74; E.T. Martin, *The Ash manuscripts, written in the year 1735, by Lieut-Col. Thomas Ash* (Belfast, 1890); Nesbitt, *Family of Nisbet*, pp 36–8; J.H. Stevenson, 'Arnold Nesbitt and the the borough of Winchelsea' *Sussex Archaeological Collections* (1991), cxxix, pp 183–93.

49 T.C. Barnard, 'The Protestant Interest, 1641–1660', in J. Ohlmeyer (ed.), *From independence to occupation: Ireland 1640–1660* (Cambridge, 1995), pp 235–40; Hayton, 'Ireland and the English ministers', pp 112–13; Hayton, 'Walpole and Ireland', in J. Black (ed.), *Britain in the age of Walpole* (London, 1984), pp. 95–119.

These political oscillations were not irrelevant to the dispute over how best the Protestant dissenters should be treated. Conolly, like others of his kinsfolk and allies, knew intimately the world of northern dissent. When first he emerged as a public figure in 1691 he had adopted the protective guise of a conformist, recommended to the second duke of Ormonde as 'a man of known integrity and ability, and a firm Protestant according to the rites of the Church of England'.[50] Subsequently, as Conolly prospered, he gained the reputation for friendliness towards the Protestant nonconformists. In particular, during the session of 1719 he backed the ending of the Test, even to the jeopardy of his career. 'His being for taking off the Test has given them [his opponents in parliament] a handle to oppose him in everything he says or proposes, tho' it be for the good of the kingdom'.[51] Judged by the strength of opposition, which obliged him to drop repeal, Conolly was thought to have miscalculated in identifying so openly with this controversial measure. In the longer term, however, his association with the cause hardly harmed him. Indeed, it may have enabled him to consolidate his hold over the northern interest. Again, though, the precise and changing relationship between Conolly as Speaker of the Irish Commons and his local and familial power bases has yet to be uncovered with any exactness. Suffice it to say here that his connections spanned a spectrum which ranged from the non-juring Robert Nelson at one extreme to the wealthy mercantile dissenters of Derry and Dublin at the other.[52] Such variegated kin and acquaintances were not unique to Conolly. Nor did they automatically induce sympathy with the dissenters' plight. Some who had moved from nonconformity to conformity or who lived environed with Presbyterians, wished to disavow their ancestry and disable the potentially troublesome. Equally, those whose knowledge of dissent depended more on second- than first-hand experience, might as a consequence exaggerate or minimize the threat. Nevertheless, it may not be entirely coincidence that the disappearance of repeal of the Test from parliamentary business after 1733 occurred so soon after Conolly's death and when Boyle's Munster squadrone had reestablished itself. Southern Munster, although it contained dissenting congregations in its main towns and pockets of Quakers scattered more widely, faced nothing like the coherent threat of Ulster Presbyterianism. As a result, rather different priorities in regard to religious policy may have prevailed.

The political threat posed by dissent, in so far as it could be distinguished from the republican and rebellious principles embedded in its teachings and history, rested as much on alarmism as on cool appraisal of the contemporary

50 BL, Add. MS 28877, f.91.
51 J. Bulkeley to J. Bonnell, 18 & 25 July 1719, NLI, PC 435.
52 R. Nelson to J. Bonnell, 13 September 1713, ibid., PC 435; fragment of letter of Mrs. K. Conolly to J. Bonnell [?1729], mentioning Dr D. Cumyng, ibid., PC 434; NA, M 6917/ 89; PRONI, D 1449/12/15, 17, 25; *Records of the General Synod of Ulster*, I, p. 476.

situation. Also, the terminology of sectaries, fanatics and presbyters was ban-
died about indiscriminately and intemperately. Squires whose electioneering
was opposed might blame 'Presbyterians' and 'Independents'. The accuracy of
these descriptions, used for example in county Sligo and Athlone, may be questioned.[53] Outside Ulster, Dublin and maybe one or two other sizeable boroughs,
dissent scarcely existed as a political power. Again, because of these variations,
the sense of the danger posed by dissenters differed across the island. In Dublin, dissent could be mobilised for political ends. Dr Jacqueline Hill has shown
how weakly represented were dissenters on the aldermanic board on the municipality even before the extra impediments raised by the Test Act.[54] Nevertheless, the capital was the one place in the kingdom where fellow-travellers,
'Church Presbyterians', who qualified themselves formally for office by occasional conformity, may have infiltrated the civic establishment. Moreover, the
capital, with its motley places of worship, afforded the best opportunities for
the uncertain and curious to drift in and out of distinct denominations, unclear
what barriers of doctrine and belief separated them.

The importance in Dublin of something which could be labelled as a dissenting interest, evident in the resistance to the New Rules in 1673–4, reap-
peared in the electoral contests of 1727–8.[55] One of the three candidates was
accused of putting himself at the head of several hundred dissenters, 'to employ
their preachers in declaring and soliciting for him'.[56] This candidate, the brother
of a bishop and by education and tastes an enlightened sophisticate, exemplified the gulf between the tolerant and the exclusive Anglicans.[57] The 'bulwark
of our Church', Alderman John Stoyte, was eulogised for maintaining the interests of the established Church of Ireland 'against all such as would oppose us
in our holy rites'.[58] Stoyte, as he battled for the Dublin seat, repudiated the

53 T. Caulfield to K. O'Hara, 9 October 1703, NLI, MS 20388; M. Smythe to W. Smythe,
    30 October 1731, NLI, PC 448.
54 J.R. Hill, 'Dublin corporation and dissent', below, Hill, 'Corporate values in Hanoverian
    Edinburgh and Dublin' in S.J. Connolly, R.A. Houston and R.J. Morris (eds.), *Con-
    flict, identity and economic development: Ireland and Scotland 1600–1939* (Preston,
    1995), pp. 120–2.
55 T.C. Barnard, 'Settling and unsettling Ireland; the Cromwellian and Williamite Revolu-
    tions' in Ohlmeyer, *From independence to occupation*, pp. 274–5; Hill, 'Dublin corpora-
    tion and dissent'.
56 *A letter to the freemen and freeholders of the city of Dublin, who are Protestants of the Church
    of Ireland as by law established* ([Dublin, 1727]); cf. BL, Add. MS 21122, ff.47, 55v.
57 W. Power and T. Sheridan to W. Howard, [1727], NLI, PC 223 (6); R. Howard to H.
    Howard, 2 & 6 January [1728], ibid., PC 227 (1); *Faulkner's Dublin Journal*, 2–6 May
    1727, 30 May–3 June 1727; T.C. Barnard, 'Learning, the learned and literacy in Ireland,
    1650–1760' in T.C. Barnard, D. Ó Cróinín and K. Simms (eds.), *'A Miracle of Learning'*
    (Aldershot, 1997).
58 *An elegy on the much lamented death of Alderman John Stoyte, Esq; member of Parliament
    for this city* (Dublin, 1728).

widespread notion 'that none are noble but country gentlemen, nor is there respect due but to such persons, as, like some of the Old Egyptian deities, grew in the fields'. Instead he equated virtue with town life and trade. Accordingly he contended that 'the freest and greatest peoples [were] those where trade was cultivated'.[59]

This episode revealed a powerful dissenting lobby within Dublin. It also suggested a battle in which ethical superiority no less than a parliamentary seat was at stake. The brilliance of the 'new light' did not invariably dazzle. Apologists of the Church of England, such as Alderman Stoyte, knowing that much of their support was concentrated in the larger towns, detected urbanity and civility in trade and urban pursuits. Thus, as Alderman Stoyte connected enthusiasm for civic virtue with support of the established church, he sketched an arena in which conformists and nonconformists would henceforward tussle.

III

We conclude, then, with the paradox that, while nonconformity in Ireland (as elsewhere) turned a more moderate and reasonable visage towards its congregations, it deepened the suspicions of its traditional opponents. We have seen how most of the open support from peers and country gentlemen for dissent had evaporated by the early eighteenth century. Covert backing, clear when dissenters were settled as workers and tenants on estates and when meeting-houses were provided for them, continued. The existence of this fifth-column of 'Church Presbyterians', its size difficult to calculate, disturbed the rigid conformists. However, the success of dissent in the most populous towns caused the worst worries. Such nervousness about the numbers and economic power of the dissenters matched the fears about the hold which industrious Catholics had established over urban trade.[60] These anxieties, unsupported other than by anecdotes, told as much of inherited prejudices as of the contemporary actuality. Urban economies, notoriously in Dublin, but also in Waterford, Cork, Derry and Belfast, responded violently to local and international crises. Into these communities, inherently unstable, flocked strangers. The established could vanish overnight and the throng of the destitute and desperate increase ominously. The tensions which resulted could express themselves in sectarianism. Depending

59 *Faulkner's Dublin Journal*, 10–14 October 1727.
60 D. Dickson, 'Catholics and Trade in eighteenth-century Ireland: an old debate revisited', in Power and Whelan, *Endurance and Emergence*, pp 85–100; Clarkson, 'Armagh 1770', p. 84. Cf. J. Seed, 'Gentlemen dissenters: the social and political meanings of rational dissent in the 1770s and 1780s', *Historical Journal* (1985), xxviii, pp. 299–325.

on the confessional mixture, papists or Protestant dissenters might be subjected to violence.[61]

Even without the excitements which might unexpectedly disturb otherwise torpid towns, generalised fears about the economy and society focused on specific denominations. Those who scrupled to join in the frequent jollifications which punctuated the civic year furnished easy targets for the mob. A Quaker in Cork in 1755 resignedly reported yet another evening when his and other Friends' windows had been smashed because they had failed to illuminate them for a municipal festivity.[62] Innocent victims of communal hysteria such dissenters might be. Yet this Quaker, like many another dissenter, did not spare his feckless neighbours for their inexorable descent down the primrose path.[63] Exuding disapproval, as well as abstaining from many of the duties of the parish and municipality, these sectaries were the more resented because successful in business. Forms of trading which no longer revolved around simple exchange of 'natural' commodities like the fruits of the earth or even specie quickened in early eighteenth-century Ireland. Hostility to transactions often barely understood, such as banking, paper-money and credit, reinforced long-standing suspicions of the dissenters.[64] The monied interest in Ireland, no less than in the City of London, was predominately conformist. Yet the prominence of the odd dissenter, together with the ecstatic embrace by some dissenting intellectuals of the worlds of goods and merchandizing, brought odium onto nonconformists. Owing to the misfortunes of the South Sea Bubble, the failure to establish a national bank in Ireland and a series of spectacular bankruptcies in Dublin, traditionalists within the established church and landed order were confirmed in an unreasoning aversion towards rich dissenters.[65] The town, although it could be presented as the seat of virtue, could relapse into its less flattering represen-

---

61 P. Fagan, 'The Dublin Catholic mob (1700–1750)', *Eighteenth-century Ireland* (1989), iv, pp. 133–42.

62 Joseph Wight's diary, 30 May & 3 June 1755, Friends' Historical Library, Dublin.

63 Ibid., 1 May 1752, 13 January & 28 March 1753, 2 December 1754, 18 February & 12 June 1755.

64 J. Hoppitt, 'Attitudes to credit in Britain 1680–1790', *Historical Journal* (1990), xxxiii, pp. 305–22; M. Ryder, 'The Bank of Ireland, 1721: land, credit and dependency', ibid., (1982), xxv, pp 557–80.

65 P. Kelly, ' "Industry and virtue versus luxury and corruption": Berkeley, Walpole and the South Sea Bubble crisis', *Eighteenth-century Ireland* (1992), vii, pp. 57–74. One dissenter implicated in the controversy which followed the collapse of Burton's Bank, for which he had acted as chief teller, was Oswald Edwards. See, *The Case of Oswald Edwards, being an impartial and faithful account of the several and great services done for the creditors of the bank lately kept by Samuel Burton and Daniel Falkiner, esqrs. and of the ill natur'd and ungenerous treatment which he has had from Robert Roberts, esq.* (Dublin, 1740); K. Herlihy, 'The Irish Baptists, 1650–1780', PhD dissertation, TCD (1992), p. 108.

tation as the sump of vices: vices associated with religious and political as well as moral deviancy.[66]

Attitudes towards dissent remained ambivalent. This was inevitable when it took so many diverse forms. In the remoter regions of Ulster, where Seceders and Covenanters thrived, it retained its old links with rebellion. Elsewhere, as in the prospering port of Derry, where this cursory survey began, conformists and dissenters coexisted. Such a situation improved on that which had prevailed in the 1670s, when the Church of Ireland bishop feared for his life if he remained in his seat, so fierce were ethnic and denominational antipathies. However, in Derry, as in other corporations, the apparent harmony was contained within a framework defined by the exclusive Test Act. If, for the moment, the public campaign to repeat the Test had been ended, and if it was now possible to appoint a Derry Presbyterian to help defend Protestant Ireland, these were no more than temporary accommodations. External and internal strains, arising from unpredictable conjunctions of economic, political and demographic movements, might upset the precarious equilibrium. So it was that the attitudes of those who made and enforced religious policy in Hanoverian Ireland veered between forbearance and vindictiveness. And so it was that the Test Act lasted so long.

In writing this essay I have been fortunate in reading as yet unpublished work by David Hayton, Ian McBride and Gerard McCoy. I am also grateful to David Hayton, Ray Gillespie and Mary Lou Legg for directing me to material which otherwise I might not have located, and to the audience in the crypt at Ely Place on the memorable evening when the original of this paper was delivered.

66 BL, Stowe MS 200, ff.235, 301, 334; NLI, MS 2505/171, 189.

Dublin Corporation, Protestant Dissent, and Politics, 1660–1800

JACQUELINE R. HILL

The role of Protestant dissenters in Dublin civic politics is not a subject that has received any sustained attention. One of the obstacles to such a study is the obscurity that still surrounds the religious composition of the corporation and its associated guilds. Historians have noted that spasmodic attempts were made to confine civic freedom to Protestants as early as the 1650s,[1] and that from the 1690s to 1793 Catholics were not admitted to freedom of guilds or to membership of the corporation. (Exclusion of Catholics from membership of Dublin corporation in fact lasted from the 1690s until the Municipal Reform Act of 1840 came into effect in 1841, altough a small number of Catholics entered the Dublin guilds in the 1790s.)[2] Protestant dissenters fared better, although they formed a small minority of the city's population: at best, in the early eighteenth century, around ten per cent, and less than twenty per cent of the Protestant element.[3] There were dissenters among the guilds and on the corporation from the 1650s onward, and studies have highlighted the role of particular dissenting groups and individuals in civic life.[4] Work in progress by the Dublin Heritage Group towards creating a data-base of Dublin's freemen will facilitate more systematic analysis of the corporation's religious composition. In the meantime, this paper offers some preliminary observations on the presence of dissenters in corporate life and discusses their political importance.

---

1 T.C. Barnard, *Cromwellian Ireland* (Oxford, 1975), p. 68.
2 See Jacqueline Hill, 'The politics of privilege: Dublin corporation and the Catholic question, 1792–1823', *Maynooth Review* (1982), vii, pp. 17–36.
3 Patrick Fagan, 'The population of Dublin in the eighteenth century with particular reference to the proportions of Catholics and Protestants', *Eighteenth-Century Ireland* (1991), vi, pp. 121–56, at pp. 134–5.
4 Barnard, *Cromwellian Ireland*, pp. 81–3. For some case studies, see Raymond Hylton, 'Dublin's Huguenot communities: trials, development, and triumph, 1662–1701', *Proceedings of the Huguenot Society of London* (1983–8), xxiv, pp. 221–31; Olive Goodbody, 'Anthony Sharp, wool merchant, 1643–1707, and the Quaker community in Dublin', *Journal of the Friends' Historical Society* (1956), xlviii, pp. 38–50.

From the time of the introduction of the 'New Rules', imposed by the crown in 1672, Dublin corporation was confirmed as a two-chamber body, consisting of a board of twenty-five aldermen who sat for life, and were self-selecting, and a lower house, or 'city commons', composed of ninety-six guild representatives and up to forty-eight sheriffs' peers (those who had served the office of sheriff or had paid a fine to be excused). The aldermen were drawn for the most part from the city's wealthiest Protestant merchants. Each year they selected from among their number the lord mayor (usually but not invariably by seniority). Their importance in corporate life was reinforced by their role in choosing the guild representatives for the city commons, from double returns supplied by the guilds.[5]

Since the aldermen constituted a powerful local oligarchy, it will be appropriate to begin by considering the dissenter presence on the aldermanic board, so far as it is known (table 1). One of the most notable features of the board during the Restoration period was the presence of pre-Cromwellian dissenters; Presbyterians and Independents. These aldermen had begun their civic careers before 1649, and their presence illustrates in the Dublin context the element of continuity from the pre- to the post-Cromwellian eras that historians have observed in the landowning and parliamentary spheres.[6] Others, including Enoch Reader and Humphrey Jervis, were admitted to freedom and began their participation in civic life only in the 1650s. In this respect it is important to note that there was no counterpart in Ireland of the English Corporation Act (1661)[7] that imposed a sacramental test on municipal office-holders. Jervis was a particularly important figure. A merchant and ship-owner, son of a Staffordshire gentleman, he is credited with establishing two Presbyterian meeting houses, one in Strand Street and the other on land formerly belonging to St Mary's Abbey, purchased from the corporation in 1675. His entrepreneurial activities (including bridge-building) interested successive viceroys, and in 1681 the duke of Ormond requested the corporation to elect Jervis lord mayor for a second term.[8]

---

5 For the working of the corporation, see Sean Murphy, 'The corporation of Dublin, 1660–1760', *Dublin Historical Record* (1984), xxxviii, pp. 22–35.
6 See, e.g., Karl Bottigheimer, 'The Restoration land settlement in Ireland: a structural view', *Irish Historical Studies* [hereafter *IHS*], (1972), xviii, pp. 1–21, at pp. 7–9.
7 13 Car. II, st. 2, c. 1.
8 Hutchison Papers, Trinity College, Dublin, MS 8556-8/231; MS 8556-8/74, 75.

Table 1 Protestant dissenter presence on (25-member) aldermanic board, 1660–87

Name	Religion	Sheriff	To Aldermanic Board	Lord Mayor	Dublin MP	Death
Dan. Hutchinson	Independent	1647 (did not serve)	1648	1652–3	1654	1675
Robert Deey	Presbyterian	?	1649	1659–60, 1672–3		?1686
Richard Tighe	Independent	1649–50	1650	1651–2, 1655–6		1656
Enoch Reader	Presbyterian?	1660 (excused)	1663	1670–1		
Humphrey Jervis	Presbyterian	1674–5	1675	1681–3		1708

Source: J.T. and R.M. Gilbert, *Calendar of ancient records of Dublin* (19 vols, Dublin, 1889–1944), iv–v.

In 1672, during a dispute over state regulation of the corporation, three of the dissenters noted in table 1 were among those who achieved notoriety when the lord mayor dismissed seven aldermen who were (perhaps unfairly) perceived as having lent their weight to the new regulations. The seven, described a year later as being 'the seven wise masters' of the then lord mayor (Presbyterian Robert Deey), and 'addicted to that [Presbyterian] faction'[9] consisted of Hutchinson, Tighe and Reader, together with four aldermen who are not known to have been dissenters themselves (table 2). The aldermen appealed against their dismissal to the royal court in London, and gained the support of the rising Presbyterian peer, the earl of Shaftesbury: they were all reinstated by order of the Irish privy council later in 1672.[10]

Table 2 The seven dismissed aldermen, 1672 (the 'Presbyterian faction')

Name	Religion	Sheriff	To Aldermanic Board	Lord Mayor	Dublin MP	Death
Hutchinson)						
Tighe) See Table 1						
Reader)						
Mark Quinn	Ch. of Ireland	?	1658	1667–8		1675
Lewis Desmynieres	"	?	1663	1669–70		
Joshua Allen	"	1664–5	1665	1673–4		
Sir Francis Brewster	"	1664–5	1665	1674–5		1704

Source: *CARD*, iv–vi.

9   Statement of 'Protestants of the Church of England', enclosed with [earl of Essex] to Lord Arlington, 19 July 1673, *Calendar of State Papers, Domestic Series, 1673*, [herafter CSPD], pp. 444–6.
10 *CSPD, 1671–2*, pp. 418–9; *CSPD, 1672*, p. 644; Dublin Corporation Archives, [hereafter DCA], Monday Book, MR/18, ff.78b–80a.

What were the political implications of the strong dissenter presence on Dublin's aldermanic board during the Restoration? If Dublin conformed to the London model, it might be expected that the corporation would display strong Whig or exclusionist sympathies in the 1670s and 1680s. There are some signs of such views. Protesting against their dismissal in 1672, the seven aldermen complained that the proposed state regulation of Dublin corporation would have reduced the city 'to more monarchical principles than their present constitution allowed of'.[11] The fact that their London contacts included Shaftesbury was significant: by 1673 he had become the chief spokesman for the 'Country' opposition in England. However, during the exclusion crisis itself (1678–81), when attempts were made in the English parliament to bring about the exclusion of James, duke of York, from the royal succession on account of his Catholicism, Dublin corporation adopted a low key and loyalist approach, failing to throw its weight behind exclusion. The explanation for this appears to lie in the management skills of the first duke of Ormond, who was reinstated as viceroy in 1677, and who soon had the corporation eating out of his hand.[12]

After a brief spell of Catholic dominance during the Jacobite era, Dublin corporation reverted in the 1690s to Protestant control. Although most of the aldermanic dissenters from the commonwealth era had died by this time, Sir Humphrey Jervis (who was knighted in the early 1680s) survived as an active member of the board until 1705, well into Queen Anne's reign.[13] So did one or two of the 'Presbyterian' group of Church of Ireland aldermen, including Sir Francis Brewster (a leading figure in parliamentary opposition in the 1690s)[14] who died in 1704, and Sir Joshua Allen (table 2). To these aldermen was added in the 1690s Thomas Bell, a Presbyterian merchant. Bell served as sheriff in Dublin, 1691–2, shortly after the revolution, and well before his term as sheriff expired he was elevated to the aldermanic board. His civic career peaked when he was chosen to be lord mayor in 1702–3, and appointed city treasurer on the expiry of his mayoralty. This high status was confirmed when in 1703 he was elected MP for Armagh town in the general election that followed Queen Anne's accession to the throne. However, after the introduction of the Sacramental Test for public

11 CPSD, 1672, pp. 127–31.
12 Jacqueline Hill, *From patriots to unionists: Dublin civic politics and Irish Protestant patriotism* (Oxford, forthcoming), chapter 2.
13 J.T. Gilbert, and R.M. Gilbert, *Calendar of the Ancient Records of Dublin* [hereafter *CARD*] (19 vols, Dublin, 1889–1944), vi, p. 340.
14 James McGuire, 'The Irish parliament of 1692', in Thomas Bartlett and D.W. Hayton (eds), *Penal era and golden age* (Belfast, 1979), pp. 113, at p. 11. Brewster, a Kerry landlord and writer on economic affairs (DNB) was MP for Tuam, 1692–1703, Doneraile, 1703–4, and a commissioner of forfeited estates. In the 1690s he was Dublin corporation's agent in London (*CARD*, v, p. 508).

office in 1704, Bell refused to take the Test (the only Dublin alderman to do so) and consequently lost his place as treasurer and alderman. He thereupon dropped out of civic life for the rest of Queen Anne's reign. In a petition to the corporation in 1715 he claimed he had experienced 'great losses by sea and land', and asked for some recompense for expenses incurred in the service of the city: he was granted an annual sum of fifty pounds.[15]

The two decades that followed the introduction of the Sacramental Test appear to have been the most barren of the entire century as far as dissenter representation on the aldermanic board was concerned. (This was not peculiar to the capital: in general the effect of the Test on Irish corporations was to remove most of the dissenters.)[16] After the withdrawal of Bell, and the retirement, c.1705, of Jervis, no dissenter has been identified on the Dublin board before the elevation of Joseph Kane in 1722. The intervening period witnessed the appointment in 1710 of a Tory ministry by Queen Anne. This ministry not only disliked dissenters, but was apt to view with suspicion even those members of the established church who did not sufficiently endorse the church's interests. A prolonged struggle between the corporation and the Irish privy council from 1711 to 1714 over the filling of the mayoral office witnessed the introduction of party labels into the language of Dublin civic politics.[17] The efforts of the privy council to exclude all but Tories from the post alienated the bulk of aldermen, and had the effect of confirming and strengthening Dublin corporation's moderately Whiggish tendencies, which had been apparent since the 1690s.[18]

With the accession of the Hanoverians in 1714, Whigs came to dominate the ministries formed in England and Ireland. Although the Sacramental Test remained in place, in 1719 limited toleration for Trinitarian dissenters in Ireland was granted through the toleration act of that year; and from 1725 onwards successive indemnity acts also took some of the sting out of the Test.[19] The first dissenter in Dublin civic politics to benefit from the more relaxed climate by being raised to the board was Joseph Kane, a merchant who had served as sheriff in 1709–10, just before the Tory regime came in, but who subsequently had to wait to become an alderman until the more favourable climate of the 1720s. His son, the Presbyterian merchant and banker Nathaniel Kane, served as sheriff in 1720–21. Kane senior reached the mayoralty in 1725–6, and on his

15 DCA, Monday Book, MR/18, ff.158a–158b; *CARD*, iv, pp. 531–2.
16 J.C. Beckett, *Protestant dissent in Ireland 1687–1780* (London, 1948), pp. 489.
17 David Hayton, 'The crisis in Ireland and the disintegration of Queen Anne's last ministry', in *IHS* (1981), xxii, pp. 193–215; Catherine M. Flanagan, ' "A merely local dispute?": partisan politics and the Dublin mayoral dispute of 1709–1715', PhD thesis, University of Notre Dame, Indiana, 1983.
18 Hill, *From patriots to unionists*, chapter 2.
19 6 George I, c. 5; for a list of indemnity acts see Beckett, *Protestant dissent in Ireland*, p. 81.

death in 1727 his son succeeded to his place on the aldermanic board, serving as lord mayor in 1734–5.[20] Thus a dissenter presence on the Dublin board resumed after only a short break.

The mayoral dispute of Queen Anne's reign had produced tensions in the corporation, but for the most part they were tensions within the aldermanic board, and the city commons played only a peripheral role. In the 1720s the two houses of the corporation were at one over the Wood's halfpence affair: like Dean Jonathan Swift, the corporation was hostile to the patent granted to Wood. Matters however changed in the 1740s, as a result of the struggles spearheaded by two members of the city commons, Charles Lucas and James Digges La Touche (a second-generation Huguenot), to overturn the aldermanic oligarchy in the corporation.[21] Although a desire on the part of the city commons to reassert 'ancient rights' was not entirely new, the selection of Lucas as a representative of his guild, the barber-surgeons, in 1741, gave added impetus to the cause. Both Lucas and La Touche (who represented the weavers' guild) were members of the established church: though Lucas later let it be known that while he conformed to the church out of sense of duty to the laws of the land, he knew of 'no Tenet, necessary to Salvation, in which I differ from the Presbiterians [*sic*]'.[22] In his view, the only substantial issue between the Presbyterians and the established church was the form of church government, which ought not to be a source of discord.

If Lucas harboured Presbyterian sympathies but remained a member of the Church of Ireland, others, who held important civic offices in the early 1740s, were less respectful of the claims of the established church. Two Presbyterians, James Dunn and Thomas Read, filled one of the two shrieval offices in 1740–1 and 1741–2 respectively. It is not entirely clear why dissenters were chosen (by the lord mayor and aldermen) for such an important post—apart from anything else, sheriffs chaired meetings of the city commons—for two years in succession. The choices may need to be seen as part of a legacy of the mayoral dispute of Queen Anne's reign. Dunn's selection coincided with the mayoralty (by seniority) of Alderman Samuel Cooke, a brewer who was the son of the Tory lord mayor who had caused much controversy by holding on to the mayoralty for a second year (1713–14).[23] It is possible that the aldermen chose a Presbyterian to be the senior or 'city' sheriff so as to demonstrate to the privy council (which was still required, under the New Rules, to approve the choice) that Cooke's mayoralty did not

---

20 *CARD*, vii, pp. 133, 310; viii, pp. 406, 422–3.
21 Sean Murphy, 'The Lucas affair: a study of municpal and electoral politics in Dublin, 1742–9', MA thesis, National University of Ireland, University College Dublin, 1981.
22 Charles Lucas, *The political constitutions of Great Britain and Ireland* (2 vols, London, 1751), ii, pp. 442–3.
23 *CARD*, vii, 521–61; ix, p. 1.

mean that the corporation was moving back in a 'Tory' direction. The following year saw the mayoralty of William Aldrich (d. 1746), who had been
repeatedly nominated for sheriff by the Whiggish aldermen during the mayoral dispute in 1711, 1712 and 1713 (and invariably rejected by the privy
council). His subsequent civic career had been slow: he served as sheriff in
1714–15, but took another seventeen years to reach the aldermanic board in
1732. His reputation as a strong Whig was confirmed when after one of the
shrieval offices became unexpectedly vacant in November 1741, he and the
aldermen chose Thomas Read, a 'New Light' Presbyterian merchant, for the
post.[24]

Thus the era of challenge to the oligarchic nature of the corporation
coincided with a dissenting presence in the shrieval office. The political
importance of the post may be judged by the subsequent fortunes of the
individuals elected to it at this period. The shrievalty was a stepping stone to
the aldermanic board, and James Dunn (whose tenure of office had ended
just before Lucas's entry to the city commons and the beginnings of serious
tensions between the two chambers) was duly elevated to the board in 1746.[25]
But of the eight individuals (including the Presbyterian Read) who filled the
office in the four years after Dunn only one was subsequently selected for
the board. This was highly unusual: in the twenty years between 1730–1 and
1749–50 at least one of the sheriffs each year, except for the period in question, was eventually raised to the board. It seems likely that this departure
from tradition in itself intensified resentments between the two chambers
and fuelled opposition to oligarchy in the later 1740s. For instance, in October 1749, on the eve of two highly contentious by-elections in the city, the
reformers faced a major setback when Charles Lucas was condemned by the
Irish house of commons as a enemy to his country, and subsequently fled to
avoid arrest. This left his supporters with only one candidate (La Touche) to
contest the two city seats, which had fallen vacant through the deaths of both
city MPs.[26] At this critical juncture it was Thomas Read who emerged as
substitute for Lucas, thus demonstrating his defiance of the aldermen, who
had blocked his prospects for rising in the city hierarchy.

Although Read failed to obtain enough votes to be elected, his candidacy
alarmed champions of the established church. For a short time talk of 'the church
in danger' was heard again; and at the poll the great majority of the Church of
Ireland clergy voted for the aldermanic candidates.[27] The repercussions for dis-

24 *CARD*, ix, p. 407.
25 *CARD*, ix, pp. 419–20. Significantly, Dunn was elected in place of Alderman Aldrich
     (deceased).
26 Sean Murphy, 'Charles Lucas and the Dublin election of 1748–1749', *Parliamentary
     History* (1983), ii, pp. 93–111.
27 Ibid., p. 106.

scntcrs in Dublin civic life did not end there. In 1750 James Dunn became eligible (by seniority) to fill the mayoral office. The prospect of a Presbyterian lord mayor, so soon after the controversial by-elections, caused divisions on the board, and Dunn's selection for the office was blocked by a majority of the aldermen. Some years later Dunn had his revenge when in 1758 he took advantage of another vacancy in the city's parliamentary representation to stand himself, having first ostentatiously resigned his place on the aldermanic board. Reform of the aldermen's oligarchic powers had still not been achieved, and Dunn was elected by 1,363 to 1,192 votes in a straight contest with the city's recorder, James Grattan. Dunn held the seat until 1761 when during the general election of that year he generously stood down in favour of Lucas, who had returned from exile on the accession of George III.[28] Dunn thus became the first Presbyterian to represent the city in parliament since the 1650s, and one of only a handful of Presbyterian MPs in Ireland.[29]

Table 3   Percentage of voters by guild casting both votes for the 'anti-oligarchical' candidates, La Touche and Read, Dublin city by-elections, 1749 (Percentage of dissenters among the voters in brackets)

75–100 per cent	*50–74 per cent*	*25–49 per cent*	*0–24 per cent*
Sheermen & Dyers (20.6)	Weavers (30.6)	Carpenters (15.3)	Bakers (5.9)
	Curriers (25.0)	Saddlers (2.9)	Cooks (3.6)
	Tanners (45.5)	Glovers (22.7)	Apothecaries (28.6)
	Hosiers (16.3)	Goldsmiths (4.5)	Brewers (0.0)
	Feltmakers (11.5)	Tailors (20.0)	
	Chandlers (32.6)	Shoemakers (11.7)	
	Joiners (7.3)	Smiths (6.6)	
	Barber-Surgeons (10.3)	Merchants (22.0)	
		Bricklayers (5.6)	
		Coopers (10.5)	
		Cutlers (12.7)	
		Butchers (2.8)	
Percentage dissenter, these voters	*Percentage dissenter, these voters*	*Percentage dissenter, these voters*	*Percentage dissenter, these voters*
7/34 = 20.6%	156/629 = 24.8%	219/1,564 = 14.0%	8/77 = 10.4%

Average dissenters in all guilds (based on those who voted, 1749) = 17.0 per cent

Note: Only 15.6 per cent of the guild voters (freemen) split their votes between 'anti-oligarchical' and aldermanic candidates, reflecting the high degree of politicisation of the voters (a further 2.5 per cent cast just one of their votes).

Source: An alphabetical list of the freemen and freeholders of the city of Dublin, who polled at the election for members of parliament (1749) (Dublin, 1750), with MS annotations concerning religion (Royal Irish Academy, Haliday pamphlets, vol. 214).

28 *CARD*, ix, pp. 439–40; *The free electors' address to Colonel Dunn, with his answer* ([Dublin, 1761]) (Cambridge Univresity Library, Bradsaw Collection, Hib. 3. 748. 1 (55)).
29 Beckett, *Protestant dissent in Ireland*, pp. 139–40.

All this suggests that there was a dissenter (or, at any rate, a Presbyterian) input into the anti-oligarchic campaigns of mid-eighteenth-century Dublin. This impression is strengthened by analysis of the election results in 1749, where (unusually) contemporary notes give an insight into the religious composition of the electorate (table 3).

However, table 3 shows that while guilds with above average proportions of dissenters among the freemen were more likely to support the anti-oligarchical candidates, the pattern was not an inflexible one. Several guilds with above average levels in fact gave less than half their votes to the reformers, including the glovers, tailors, merchants, and apothecaries. Similarly, the feltmakers, joiners, and barber-surgeons (Lucas's guild) had well below average proportions of dissenters, but still gave over half their votes to La Touche and Read. Moreover, there were other factors influencing voting choices in this election. It has been argued elsewhere that support for the anti-oligarchical candidates was strongest among the textile trades, and among those trades that processed cattle products.[30] In any case, it should be noted that one of Lucas's main targets for attack on the aldermanic board for allegedly failing to defend the real interests of the city was Alderman Nat Kane, himself a Presbyterian.[31]

The spectacle of dissenters contesting and (in Dunn's case) winning a Dublin city parliamentary seat, plus the appearance in 1760 of a measure of

Table 4   Dissenters among guild nominations to city commons, 1759
(selection made by aldermen from double returns)

Guild	Dissenters among nominees	Dissenters selected by aldermen
Tailors	2/8	0
Butchers	1/6	0
Shoemakers	2/8	0
Weavers	2/6	0
Coopers	1/4	0
Hosiers	2/4	?1 (page torn)
Brewers	2/8	1

No dissenters nominated by smiths, carpenters, saddlers, tanners, chandlers, glovers, sheermen, goldsmiths, feltmakers, cutlers, curriers, joiners, apothecaries; no information for merchants, cooks, bricklayers, bakers and barber-surgeons.

Source: as table 3. Twelve years earlier in 1747 there were as many as ten dissenters on the corporation (including aldermen) (Murphy, 'The Lucas affair', p. 30).

30 Hill, *From patriots to unionists*, chapter 4.
31 See Anon. [Charles Lucas], *An eighteenth address to the free-citizens and free-holders of the city of Dublin* (Dublin, 1749), pp. 39, 47-9.

corporation reform,[32] may have made the board wary about selecting dissenters either as guild representatives, or for promotion in the civic hierarchy. A snapshot survives from this period of the religion of guild nominees for the lower house, and of those selected by the aldermen (table 4).

The figures in table 4 show a substantial dissenter presence among guild nominees, but it is not clear how typical this was. The dissenter profile in Dublin was very high in 1759, for James Dunn was at that time one of the city MPs: this may have encouraged guilds to put forward dissenters for the city commons.

Following the death of Nat Kane in 1756 and the resignation of James Dunn in 1758 it appears that more than a decade passed without any dissenter being elected to the board. However, the methods of selection of officials had changed as a result of the 1760 act. From henceforth sheriffs were to be selected by the aldermen from a panel of eight freemen who had received most votes in the city commons. Aldermen (who still had to have served the shrieval office or paid a fine to be excused) were to be selected by the city commons from among four sheriffs' peers nominated by the aldermen. The first dissenter to reach the board under the new system was the Presbyterian merchant Patrick Boyd, who was chosen to be sheriff in 1767–8 and elevated to the board in 1772. When his turn came to serve the mayoralty, however, he requested to be excused, and this was granted.[33]

The main effect of corporation reform and the new participation by the city commons in the task of choosing sheriffs was to make it more common for dissenters to serve the shrieval office (it should however also be noted that the Sacramental Test in Ireland was repealed in 1780). Between 1761 and 1792 at least six dissenters in addition to Boyd either filled the office or paid fines to be excused. They included the Quaker merchant Edward Strettel, who in 1774 paid a very large sum of two hundred pounds to be excused. The others (who all served the office) were Presbyterians: William Alexander (sheriff, 1776–7); David Dick (1781–2); Brent Neville (1787–8); Benjamin Gault (1791–2), and Henry Hutton (1792–3).[34] Inevitably, and bearing in mind that the selection of both sheriffs and aldermen was shared between the two chambers, not all these individuals reached the aldermanic board. Of those who did, the most influential was William Alexander, a wholesale merchant who became an alderman in 1779. Indeed, it was he who was partly responsible for promoting fellow Presbyterians in the civic hierarchy. Thus it

32 Dublin City Corporation Act (33 George II, c. 16). See Sean Murphy, 'The corporation of Dublin', pp. 32–3.
33 *CARD*, xii, p. 165; xiii, pp. 1, 13–4.
34 Ibid., xii, pp. 319, 418; xiii, pp. 175; xiv, pp. 9, 196, 266.

was during his mayoral year (1787–8) that Neville filled the shrieval office; and in the 1790s at least one loyalist and government confidant, Francis Higgins, expressed concern at Alderman Alexander's efforts to boost the number of Presbyterians on the board (Hutton became an alderman in 1796).[35]

Higgins' concern about the possibility of a 'Presbyterian party' on the board has to be evaluated in the context of the political disturbances of the 1790s, and particularly the spread of the United Irishmen among Ulster dissenters in 1796 and 1797.[36] By 1796 Higgins clearly doubted the loyalty of certain Dublin Presbyterians. However, although Dublin corporation contained a small complement of United Irishmen, dissenters were not prominent among them. The most important was the iron founder Henry Jackson, who was returned to the city commons as a representative of the merchants' guild in 1790 and again in 1793.[37] Most dissenters on Dublin corporation were not United Irishmen, and appear to have taken little part in politics, though Henry Hutton did agree to chair a reform meeting in Dublin during his shrieval year in 1793.[38]

Before the 1790s one of the most politically influential dissenters in Dublin was Travers Hartley, a merchant who represented his guild on the city commons in 1762. Hartley never served as sheriff, though he was included on the panel of nominees in rather unusual circumstances in 1763.[39] His main sphere of action in the 1760s was the committee of merchants, and he was also a founder member of the first Dublin chamber of commerce in 1783: these bodies contained Catholics as well as dissenters and members of the established church.[25] Like James Dunn in 1758, Hartley showed that in the second half of the century it was not necessary to be either an alderman or in the established church[40] to win a Dublin city parliamentary seat. The politicisation of the freemen in the 1740s and 1750s meant that aldermen no longer enjoyed a virtual monopoly of the city representation, and Hartley won a city seat in 1782 and held it until 1790.[41]

On the aldermanic board a dissenter presence survived down to the 1820s (Alderman Alexander died in 1822). By that time the corporation was becoming increasingly polarised over the issue of Catholic emancipation, and partici-

35 Higgins to Edward Cooke, 14 September 1796, National Archives, Rebellion Papers, 620/18/14.
36 Nancy J. Curtin, *The United Irishmen: popular politics in Ulster and Dublin, 1791–1798* (Oxford, 1994), chapter 3.
37 R.B. McDowell, 'The personnel of the Dublin Society of United Irishmen, 1791–4' *IHS* (1940–1), ii, pp. 12–53, at p. 36; *CARD*, xiv, pp. 545, 547.
38 Hill, *From patriots to unionists*, chapter 9.
39 *CARD*, xi, pp. 463–6.
40 L.M. Cullen, *Princes & pirates: the Dublin chamber of commerce 1783–1983* (Dublin, 1983), chapters 3 and 4.
41 Ibid., p. 35.

pation by prominent dissenters appears to have fallen away. However, in the absence of a systematic study of the religious composition of the lower house it is not possible to say for certain that the dissenting presence was reduced. There were several evangelical Protestants on the board and on the city commons from the late eighteenth century onwards, and these included at least one Methodist.[42]

This paper has focused principally on dissenters who reached the aldermanic board, the pinnacle of power as far as Dublin civic politics was concerned. For the most part it has not attempted to identify those aldermen who were not, apparently, dissenters themselves, but who had strong family links with dissenters, such as Daniel Falkiner and his son-in-law Benjamin Geale, whose connections were with the Baptists. These individuals are of interest, but they lie outside the scope of the present paper. It remains to make some general points about dissenter presence in the corporation during this period. There was a small but significant dissenter presence on the aldermanic board in Dublin for virtually the entire period, 1660–1800. The main exceptions were in the years immediately after the introduction of the Sacramental Test in 1704 and in the 1760s, following James Dunn's defiance of the aldermen and capture of a city parliamentary seat in 1758. It is noteworthy that all the dissenters who reached the board were Presbyterians. That is scarcely surprising. Presbyterians represented Dublin's largest Protestant dissenting group; unlike the Quakers, they had no scruples about taking oaths (and to rise in the civic hierarchy meant taking many oaths). What of the political implications of their presence? While it is clear that Presbyterians could and did contribute, as corporation members or simply as freemen of the guilds, to anti-oligarchical pressures during the eighteenth century, it would be stretching the evidence to suggest that they were invariably a force for change. Many individuals served as sheriffs or as aldermen without, apparently, disturbing their Church of Ireland colleagues. It should also be borne in mind that, with occasional exceptions of state pressure being brought to bear after the Restoration, these dissenters rose in the civic hierarchy because they were acceptable to the majority of aldermen. Indeed, perhaps what these findings hint at more than anything else is the predominantly harmonious relations that must have existed for much of the period between Dublin Presbyterians and members of the established church. This is an area where more research is needed, but in the absence of generally good relations it is hard to see why any dissenters should have been chosen to share in the city honours.

I should like to thank those who took part in the discussion following this paper for their helpful comments.

42 Hill, *From patriots to unionists*, chapter 13.

Ormond and Presbyterian Nonconformity, 1660–63

JAMES MCGUIRE

Among historians of Restoration Ireland the general perception of Ormond's policy towards presbyterians in Ulster has been benign. As Lady Burghclere wrote: 'By temperament and conviction alike, Ormonde was ever in favour of toleration, and in this instance [i.e. the early 1660s] he also realised that it was imperative not to drive the northern presbyterians to desperation'. Similarly Richard Bagwell believed that Presbyterians in Ulster met with 'little interference' from Ormond 'who was not naturally intolerant'. In his early work on the treatment of protestant dissent, R. Dudley Edwards saw Ormond's arrival as viceroy in 1662 as beginning a more tolerant policy of connivance at dissenter religious practice, though the later Edwards seemed to modify this perception. Likewise, in a survey of state attitudes to nonconformity published in 1987, I argued that Ormond's period in office in the 1660s was 'marked by a generally tolerationist attitude'.[1]

Paradoxically, views of a moderate Ormond rest in large measure on the testimony of the first historian of Irish Presbyterianism, Patrick Adair, himself a participant in the events he describes. Adair generally exonerates Ormond from blame for Presbyterian suffering, placing it instead on the bishops. The reasons for this are not clear, though they may lie as much in Ormond's personal courtesy to Adair, whenever they met, as in a Presbyterian desire to blame the Church of Ireland for its misfortunes. Few historians since Adair have questioned the consensus on Ormond's policies and motives, though Beckett and Connolly have

---

1 Lady Burghclere, *The life of James first duke of Ormonde 1610–1688* (London, 1912), ii, p. 54; Richard Bagwell, *Ireland under the Stuarts* (3 vols, London, 1909–16), iii, p. 325; R.D. Edwards, 'The history of the laws against Protestant nonconformity in Ireland from the Restoration (1660) to the Declaration of Indulgence (1687)', MA thesis, National University of Ireland, University College Dublin, 1932, p. 89; McGuire, 'Government attitudes to religious nonconformity in Ireland 1660–1719' in C.E.J. Caldicott, H. Gough & J-P Pettion (eds.), *The Huguenots and Ireland: anatomy of an immigration* (Dublin, 1987), pp. 258–9.

made telling comments about the thrust of policy in the early 1660s.[2] More recently Richard Greaves has emphasised Ormond's anxieties about security.[3]

If one looks more closely at the years 1660–63, this constant restatement of Ormond's fundamental tolerance seems to inhibit an understanding of both policy itself and of Ormond's role in its making (not to speak of an understanding of his personal attitude to those who dissented from the established church). This article will focus on three areas where Ormond played a significant or decisive part in 1660–63 touching on the interests of Ulster Presbyterians. The first was his role in 1660 in the appointment of what might loosely be called neo-Laudian clergy to dioceses with large Presbyterian populations. Secondly there was his unsympathetic response, after his arrival as viceroy in 1662, to the petitions of ejected Presbyterian ministers, and thirdly there was his use of the security crisis of 1663 to arrest and then contemplate the deportation of virtually all Presbyterian ministers in Ulster.

I

A few days after Charles II's triumphant return to London, Ormond ceased to be Lord Lieutenant of Ireland, the nominal position he had enjoyed in exile during the 1650s. But so far as influence and policy were concerned, this change mattered little. Indeed he was arguably more influential in the months immediately following the restoration of the monarchy than at any other stage in his long political career.[4] This was an influence which extended into most aspects of royal policy, not least Ireland. He attended the privy council regularly and, significantly for Irish policy, headed the list of names on the council's newly appointed 'committee for Irish affairs'.[5] It was to this committee that the representatives of the Dublin convention presented on 21 June their request that 'the Church of Ireland be resettled in doctrine, discipline and worship' as it had been in Charles I's reign.[6] This submission, which gives every impression of having been carefully stage managed, allowed those sympathetic to an immediate episcopal

2   W.D. Killen (ed.), *A true narrative of the rise and progress of the Presbyterian church in Ireland* ... (Belfast, 1866), passim; J.S. Reid, *History of the Presbyterian church in Ireland* (Belfast, 1867), ii, 281–2; J.C. Beckett, *The making of modern Ireland 1603–1923* (London, 1966), pp 125–9; S.J. Connolly, *Religion, law, and power. The making of Protestant Ireland 1660–1760* (London, 1992), pp. 24 et seq.

3   Richard L. Greaves, ' "That's no good religion that disturbs government": the Church of Ireland and the nonconformist challenge, 1660–88' in Alan Ford et al. (eds), *As by law established. The Church of Ireland since the reformation* (Dublin, 1995), pp 123–4.

4   J.C. Beckett, *The cavalier duke. A life of James Butler 1st duke of Ormond 1610–1688* (Belfast, 1990), pp 74–6.

5   PRO, London, PC2/55/ii.

6   TCD, MS 808, ff.156–8.

settlement of the church, of whom Ormond was the most powerful, to press for
the filling of the vacant bishoprics.[7] The names of the new bishops were com-
mon knowledge by the end of June, some weeks before a deputation from the
Synod of Ballymena arrived in London on what was to be a fruitless mission.
They had come with instructions to petition the king for a church settlement in
Ireland based on the Covenant, the Directory of Worship and the Westminster
Confession of Faith, but were told by their most influential supporter, Sir John
Clotworthy, that they would only get to see the king if they modified substan-
tially their demands.[8]

If Ormond played a significant role in having the episcopal vacancies filled
informally so soon after the Restoration (and it must be said that the evidence is
compelling though largely circumstantial), he played an even more significant
part in shaping the character of the restored episcopate by having Bishop
Bramhall's recommendations accepted. Of particular importance to this paper
were those clerics whom Bramhall nominated for dioceses with large concentrations of Scots Presbyterians: Robert Leslie (whom Patrick Adair in his narrative would single out for particular opprobrium for his treatment of Presbyterians) was initially appointed to Dromore, and subsequently to Raphoe; George
Wild and Jeremy Taylor, both Laudian clerics with a particular dislike for Presbyterianism, were appointed to Derry and Down & Connor respectively, while
Bramhall himself went to Armagh. It may be that Bramhall thought Taylor, the
author of the *Liberty of prophesying*, would be a conciliatory figure in Down &
Connor, but I think not. With his experience of Ulster in the 1630s Bramhall
knew what the new bishops must face. The following year, when the embattled
Taylor tried to get out of his purgatory in Down, Bramhall was unwilling to
oblige. The work for 'which he was sent' must be in 'some measure' completed,
'the reformation of that schismatical part of the country'. In other words his
appointment was not simply an act of patronage but of policy, and a policy with
which Ormond was closely identified.

Bramhall's visitation of the Armagh province in August 1661, during which
the primate insisted on evidence of episcopal ordination and the use of the Book
of Common Prayer, was preceded and followed by diocesan visitations to the
same purpose by Bishops Leslie, Wild and Taylor. This activity, in particular
Jeremy Taylor's refusal to debate with Presbyterian ministers on their terms
and his insistence on treating them as individuals to be picked off one by one,
left the Scots ministers predictably bitter, but it succeeded to the extent that an

7   McGuire, 'Policy and patronage: the appointment of bishops, 1660–61' in Alan Ford
     et al. (eds), *As by law established.*, p. 118; McGuire, 'The Dublin convention, the
     Protestant community and the emergence of an ecclesiastical settlement in 1660' in
     Art Cosgrove and J.I. McGuire (eds), *Parliament & community* (Belfast, 1983), pp.
     137–9.
8   Reid, *Presbyterian church*, ii, 248–53.

episcopally ordained parish clergy was in place in Presbyterian Ulster by early 1662.[9] The success of the policy owed much to the determination and single mindedness of Bramhall and his fellow bishops, but it rested too on encouragement from the civil power throughout 1661. The bishops' activities were preceded by the Lords Justices proclamation of 22 January 1661 against 'sundry unlawful assemblies ... held by papists, presbyterians, independents, anabaptists, quakers and other fanatical persons meeting in great numbers'. Parliamentary endorsement followed soon after when both houses of the Irish Parliament condemned the Solemn League and Covenant and declared for episcopal church government and the use of the Book of Common Prayer. At the same time a Presbyterian delegation from the north found little encouragement when they attempted to petition a parliament whose views seemed to parallel, even anticipate, those of the newly elected Cavalier Parliament in England.[10]

But the similarities between the English and Irish situations were deceptive. In England Presbyterians were small in number, arguably more open to accommodation, and easier to penalise.[11] Presbyterians in Ulster were overwhelmingly Scots, numerically predominant and unprepared to compromise on liturgy and episcopacy. Their ministers had been ejected from their benefices but not from Ulster and were continuing to perform their pastoral duties either discreetly or, in the case of some youthful enthusiasts, openly and defiantly in field conventicles.[12] The problem for the civil and ecclesiastical authorities was to decide how nonconformity on this scale in Ulster, against a background of overwhelming Catholic nonconformity in Ireland as a whole, should be approached.

In the months leading up to Ormond's going over to Dublin in July 1662, there were signs of a growing divergence between the Lords Justices, Orrery in particular, and the bishops on further enforcement of uniformity. Both sides recognised the scale of the problem but drew different conclusions about the likelihood of finding a solution. Asked by the Lords Justices for their views on the 'distracted condition of the church and best expedients to procure and preserve unity and uniformity', eight bishops, including Primate Bramhall, James Margetson and Henry Jones, signed a joint submission which argued, rather improbably, that an enforcement of the law could indeed counter widespread nonconformity. Suspensions of the law and dispensations might be 'available'

9 F.R. Bolton, *The Caroline tradition of the Church of Ireland* (London, 1958), pp. 33–5; Reid, *Presbyterians* church ii, 260–70

10 *Cal. S.P., Ire. 1660–62*, p. 191; Reid, *Presbyterian church*, ii, 272–6.

11 A. Browning (ed.), *English historical documents 1660–1714* (London, 1953), p. 413; I.M. Green, *The re-establishment of the Church of England 1660–1663* (Oxford, 1978), pp. 7 et seq.

12 W. Petty, *The political anatomy of Ireland* (London, 1691), pp. 8, 97; Reid, *Presbyterian church*, ii, 276–9.

in some cases and 'in some places' (unidentified), but the bishops were ada-
mant that 'in this case and in this place where we abound with papists,
presbyterians, independents of all sorts, anabaptists and quakers ... who would
equally claim the same indulgence, it were in vain to expect it'. There was 'but
one way to be offered for a full settlement, that is obliging of all men to the
known and ancient laws'. The government should let it be known that persons
not conforming 'must expect upon the first breach a vigorous execution of the
laws of the land'. As for nonconforming ministers, the Lords Justices should
seek from each bishop a list of 'seducers' in his diocese, whom justices of the
peace might admonish to conform or 'leave the soil, and go where the laws are
more favourable to them'.[13]

Despite having backed the bishops over the ejection of Presbyterian ministers from benefices in 1661, the mercurial Orrery was not convinced in early
1662 that it was possible to proceed to a policy of imposed conformity on the
populace as a whole. In April 1662 he analysed the problem for Ormond, by
now Lord Lieutenant but still in London, in a manner which rehearsed with
characteristic insight the relative dangers of enforcement or indulgence, but
which revealed also the extent of his own scepticism at the state's capacity to
require obedience to the ecclesiastical settlement:

> If the laws be fully put in execution, ten parts of eleven of the people
> will be dissatisfied; if they be not put in execution, the church will be
> dissatisfied, and sects and heresies continued, I doubt, for ever; and if
> any of the sects be indulged, it will be partiality not to indulge to all; if
> none be favoured, it may be unsafe. This is to me a short state of the
> case, and too true a one. If England and Scotland fall roundly upon the
> papists and nonconformists, and we do not, Ireland will be the sink to
> receive them all. If they are fallen upon equally in the three kingdoms,
> may not they all unite to disturb the peace?

Knowing that the Viceroy would soon be in Dublin Orrery was not prepared to recommend a particular course of action but to wait on the event; that
was Ormond's problem: 'your grace's judgement ... is most requisite for our
guidance'.[14]

Ormond's approach to Presbyterian nonconformity became clear in the
weeks following his arrival in late July 1662. He resisted attempts by Lord
Massereene to devise what Patrick Adair called 'some overtures which ... might
be a favour to non-conformists', but agreed after some delay to meet a delega-

---

13 Bodleian Library, Carte MSS, f. 53.
14 *A collection of the state letters of ... Roger Boyle, the first earl of Orrery ...* (2 vols, Lon-
    don, 1743), i, p. 109; Reid, *Presbyterian church*, ii, p. 281.

tion on 30 September consisting of three moderate Presbyterian ministers, Adair, Andrew Stuart and William Semple , accompanied by Massereene.[15] This delegation presented Ormond with a petition for 'liberty of conscience and to preach the gospel' under the king's protection. They based their case on two royal statements of 1660. The first of these was the declaration of Breda, with its promise of 'liberty to tender consciences, and that no man shall be disquieted or called in question for differences of opinion in matter of religion which do not disturb the peace of the kingdom'. The second was the official response of June 1660 to the commissioners from the Dublin convention, who had included in their submission on the ecclesiastical settlement (the ninth) the declaration of Breda's reference to liberty of conscience: 'His majesty will give direction that what is desired in the 9th proposition shall be accordingly performed'. The ministers' accurate knowledge of the response in council, which was not widely circulated in the way the Breda declaration had been, suggests that their petition was prepared under the guidance of one of their prominent backers, most likely Massereene or Montgomery.[16]

There was no immediate response on 30 September to the petitioners. Ormond is alleged, however, to have remarked the following day to Massereene and Montgomery that these ministers 'had suffered for the king, and now they were likely to suffer under the king'. He subsequently had a set of questions prepared for them to answer which included their scruples with Church of Ireland ordination and liturgy, and the identity of those for whom they spoke. The ministers response was honest and direct: in doctrine they accepted the Thirty-nine Articles of the Church of England and the Irish articles of 1615 (they did not, of course, mention the articles incorporated under Laud's and Bramhall's influence in the Irish canons of 1634–5). As for liturgy, they 'were not clear' to use the forms or ceremonies prescribed by the Book of Common Prayer; nor, more significantly, would they ever consent to any compromise which would require ministers ordained according to Presbyterian rites to be reordained by bishops.[17] These answers, together with their earlier petition, were debated in a meeting of the Irish council, at which the bishops railed predictably against the Presbyterians, though Ormond was said to have spoken moderately.[18]

15 Reid, *Presbyterian church*, ii, 283; see also Carte MSS 45, ff 449–50, 451, 452.
16 Carte MSS 45, f.462; McGuire, 'Dublin convention', p. 137.
17 Reid, *Presbyterian church*, ii, 284–5.
18 Ibid., 285.

II

Ormond's response to the Presbyterian delegation came eventually on 21 October. In a carefully worded and formal statement of policy, he reminded the petitioners that the Declaration of Breda promised a liberty to tender consciences which did 'not disturb the peace of the kingdom, those being the very words of his majesty's said declaration'. As for the convention's submission and the king's response in June 1660, from which the petitioners had again quoted the Breda reference to tender consciences, Ormond once more enlarged on the original, reminding the petitioners that the convention had in the same paragraph asked that the Church of Ireland be 'resettled in doctrine, discipline and worship' as it was in Charles I's reign, 'according to the laws then and now in force in this kingdom'. The principle of a liberty to tender consciences was acknowledged, but the practice must conform to the laws of the land. There was nothing in the king's promise from which it could be deduced that 'any man should pretend to a liberty contrary to law to assume the office of a public preacher in any diocese without special licence from the lord archbishop or bishop of the diocese'. Nevertheless, and this was Ormond's only concession to the spirit of Breda,

> in regard of HM said gracious indulgence ... we intend not that they should be hindered from exercising (in a quiet and peaceable manner) any pious duties in their own private houses to their own families or others that may occasionally lodge in their houses.

But this indulgence was not to be an excuse for any other persons to assemble publicly at a minister's house. He then went on to condemn specifically the 'erecting of pretended religious houses or public meeting places under colour of the worship of God', the holding of both public and private conventicles which might be dangerous to government, 'conduce to novelties or alteration', or disturb the public peace. Towards the end of a statement which offered the most minimal concessions to Presbyterian ministers and their immediate families, but not to Presyterians as a body, Ormond reiterated unambiguously the requirement for conformity:

> And we do hereby require the said persons to conform themselves to the laws of the land, and forbear to exercise any church discipline or ecclesiastical jurisdiction not warranted by those laws, and submit themselves as they ought to the archbishops and bishops of the dioceses wherein they live.[19]

19 Bodleian, Carte MSS 45, f.462.

Ormond's declaration of 21 October is sometimes seen as a considerable tolerationist gesture towards Presbyterians; in reality, it offered less security to Irish nonconformity, and Presbyterians in particular, than the allegedly more harsh restrictions enacted in England in the same period under the so-called Clarendon code. In a follow-up move some weeks later Ormond issued a proclamation reiterating the proclamation of 22 January 1661 banning conventicles and meetings of nonconformists.[20]

Charles II's Declaration of Indulgence, issued on 26 December 1662, applied only to England. To nonconformists in Ireland, however, it offered yet another opportunity to lobby for amelioration of the laws.[21] A Presbyterian delegation once more waited on Ormond on 25 March 1663 and offered reasons for indulgence, but the time could hardly have been less propitious to seek toleration from a Lord Lieutenant who at the best of times regarded the loyalty of Scots Presbyterians as decidedly doubtful; the discovery earlier in the same month of an apparent plot to overthrow the government, the first of the two 1663 plots, made the security situation of paramount concern.

It was the second of these plots, misleadingly known as 'Blood's plot', which was used by government to compromise Ulster Presbyterians. Ormond in Dublin and Orrery in Cork had learnt some time in March or early April that plans by a group of conspirators, including army officers, MPs and some nonconforming ministers, to seize Dublin castle and other strategic points around the country were maturing and that an attempt was to be made in May.[22] Orrery's first inclination was to round up all known 'fanatics' since 'if a fire be kindled none knew how far it might burn'. Ormond, however, decided that the conspirators' plans should be allowed to mature: 'my greatest care is not to let the conspirators find they are discovered lest they should desist and I want evidence and matter sufficient to make examples of them'.[23] This stratagem almost misfired when the conspirators decided to bring forward their seizure of Dublin Castle.[24] On the eve of the attempt, realising that their plot was discovered they decided to disperse the next day, in the hopes of reassembling soon after. In this they were foiled and twenty-four conspirators were arrested as they attempted to leave Dublin, though at least ten others managed to escape.

This conspiracy is generally and unjustifiably referred to as 'Blood's plot', but it is unlikely that Thomas Blood, an army officer with a small land holding near Dunboyne, was either an instigator or a principal participant in the conspiracy. Apart from an adventurous streak, manifest in his later career, a reason

20 *Cal. S.P., 1660–62*, p. 615; Edwards, 'Nonconformity', pp. 96–7.
21 Edwards, 'Non-conformists', pp. 99–100.
22 R. L. Greaves, *Deliver us from evil: the radical underground, 1660–1663* (New York, 1986), pp. 141 et seq.
23 *Cal S.P. Ire., 1663–1665*, p. 92.
24 *Cal. Clar. S.P.*, v. 314.

for his involvement may lie in his relationship through marriage with one of the
chief conspirators, William Leckey, a Presbyterian minister. After their arrest it
was against Leckey, Colonel Edward Warren, Captain Thomson and Colonel
Alexander Jephson that the government was able to accumulate the most telling
evidence.

What were the conspirators objectives? In a Declaration to be promulgated
on seizing the castle, they announced that they stood

> for the liberty of conscience proper to everyone of us as a Christian, for
> the establishing of the Protestant religion in purity according to the tenor
> of the Solemn League and Covenant, the restoring to each person his
> lands as he held them in 1659, the discharging the army's arrears, the
> repairing [of] the breaches made upon the liberties and privileges of the
> corporations in the three kingdoms, in all which we doubt not but the
> Lord of Hosts, the mighty God of Jacob, will strengthen our week hands'.

In other words they wished to undo the Restoration settlement in church and
state.

The trials of those conspirators against whom there was sufficient evidence
began early in July. Those charged were Leckey, the Presbyterian minister,
Thomson, Jephson and Warren. The jury, according to Ned Vernon, an army
colonel responsible for Ormond's intelligence gathering, consisted of 'discreet
persons of good estates'. In the case against Leckey one of the crown witnesses
was, again in Vernon's words, 'a most handsome woman, who with very great
soberness and more prudence than usual in that sex informed the court that she
was with Mrs Leckey ... when the troops came to search for her husband and
that Mrs Leckey expressed great fear that the attack on Dublin castle had been
discovered'; apparently Mrs Leckey was cheered by the belief that her husband
would eventually be pardoned through the good offices of two unnamed persons, inferred, according to Vernon to be Sir Audley Mervin, the speaker of the
House of Commons, and Lord Massereene (formerly Sir John Clotworthy),
since 1660 the most senior in rank of the Presbyterian lobbyists and advisor to
Adair and his fellow ministers.[25]

All four were condemned to death, though Leckey feigned madness and
avoided execution on that account for some time, at one stage escaping from
gaol. The others were executed on 15 July, each of them delivering or making
available, through the cleric who attended them, a last speech. Thomson was
said to have died like a true Christian, praying for the king and declaring himself a Church of England man, but Warren and Jephson, despite having prom-

25 *Cal. S.P. Ire., 1663–1665*, pp. 157–8.

ised to confess their guilt and exhort the people to loyalty, obedience and the renunciation of popery, in fact 'declared their seditious thoughts'.[26]

At the trial of those who were executed much was made of their avowal of the Solemn League and Covenant in their intended Declaration. At the same time the correspondence of those in government becomes increasingly peppered with references to the discovered plot as a Presbyterian conspiracy.[27] Was it in any sense a Presbyterian plot? Certainly the conspirators themselves had claimed that should they succeed, massive support might be expected from the Presbyterians of Ulster who were suffering at the hands of the restored episcopate. In a very limited sense, therefore, it was a Presbyterian plot but not one in which a majority of Presbyterians was engaged, nor was it one that a majority could be guaranteed to support, at least in the initial stages. Had the conspirators plans gathered momentum, it is arguable that Presbyterian support might have been forthcoming on a large scale. In the early months of 1663, in the aftermath of Ormond's firm line in October, Presbyterian political activity had been noticeable. According to an Ormond informant a petition, signed by many hundreds of men, had been circulating in Ulster in February. Intended for presentation to the House of Commons it complained of the persecution of Presbyterian ministers and mass excommunications. And, as previously mentioned, a delegation of Presbyterian ministers had sought in April the extension to Ireland of Charles II's Declaration of Indulgence. In other words, Presbyterians were far from contented and far from quiescent in their subjection to episcopacy. None of this amounts to the May plot being a broad based Presbyterian conspiracy but it does suggest that there existed considerable potential for growing Presbyterian support for a coup d'état that was showing every chance of succeeding.

It was, however, some three weeks after the discovery of the plot that Ormond decided to take drastic action against Presbyterian ministers in Ulster. On 16 June he sent direction for a round-up of ministers, not to the civil authorities, as Orrery had decreed the previous year, but to the bishops:

> We ... pray and require your lordships with all convenient speed to cause all such ministers or pretended ministers that you shall find cause to suspect (either to have had any hand in the said late conspiracy or to be likely by their proceedings or otherwise, to seduce the people from their due obedience and subjection to HM authority, ecclesiastical or civil within this realm) to be apprehended and committed to safe custody until further directions from us.[28]

---

26 Bodleian, Carte MSS 68, ff.574, 576–8.
27 *Cal. S.P. Ire., 1663–1665*, pp. 137–8; Bodleian, Carte MSS 32, ff.551, 566.
28 HMC, *Ormond MSS* (new series), iii, 57–8.

This led to a wholesale detention of nonconforming ministers, particularly in Ulster. The task was performed with alacrity by Robert Leslie in Raphoe, and George Wild in Derry. In Jeremy Taylor's case I have come across complaints of seditious activities by nonconforming ministers but no actual details of arrests.

What decided Ormond to act? Was it simply a perceived need to give more substance to the discovery of the May plot? Or was it a real fear that Presbyterian ministers posed a potential or real threat to the Restoration settlement in church and state? And what role did his personal antipathy to Presbyterianism play?

III

Ormond took this drastic step after he had received a report from the bishop of Kildare, via the archbishop of Dublin, that a Mr Thomson, a former Presbyterian minister and now a conforming clergyman, had reported seditious meetings to be taking place in Ulster. Ormond asked to see Thomson and within days the round-up order had gone out; more than seventy ministers were arrested.[29] He later explained his purposes:

> It is evident that whilst some unconformable silenced ministers are permitted to live in the north the people will never be brought to conformity, and will always be dangerous, and it is certain, though it cannot be judicially proved, that they were very active in the contrivance of the late design.[30]

By the end of June with most Presbyterian ministers under arrest, Ormond and the privy council issued a proclamation reviving an indulgence to the nonconforming laity, which promised that there would be no prosecutions for offences against the law of uniformity of common prayer and church attendance before 24 December.[31] The proclamation made clear that this indulgence was granted in circumstances where several ministers or pretended ministers had been arrested and were no longer in a position to seduce the people from conformity, as they had done in the past, and because the people themselves had not been drawn into the recently discovered plot; the indulgence did not extend to ministers. In other words the Presbyterian plot was a ministers' plot and the government wished to distinguish between the people and their ministers. The

29 Bodleian, Carte MSS 32, f.655.
30 *Cal. S.P. Ire., 1663–1665*, pp. 149.
31 Ibid., pp. 154–5.

latter were to be regarded as irredeemably unconformable, the former might yet comply and should be treated therefore with moderation and tact. In reality the delay of over a month in rounding up the Presbyterian ministers suggests that government knew that this was not a Presbyterian conspiracy, but that it suited Dublin Castle to treat it as such.

With hindsight we know that this strategy did not work. It foundered on the problem of what to do with the detained ministers. To Ormond's suggestion that they might be deported, Secretary Bennet replied firmly that 'the king did not desire the factious ministers to be sent to England or Scotland. Both countries already abound in them. You should think of some other expedient'. This was not very helpful for Ormond, and he was soon forced to order that most of them be released.[32]

By the end of the year policy had changed and Ormond was telling the king that the state of the country made it 'not wise to exercise the utmost severity of the law'.[33] But this change of policy was forced by circumstances. Security, lack of support from Whitehall and the sheer concentration of Scots Presbyterians in Ulster meant that policy must conform to reality. The imposition of conformity in Ireland, a plausible policy for English conditions, had been urged on Ormond by the bishops. The possibility of success had seemed briefly within his grasp in the wake of the 1663 plot; but the opportunity it offered was illusory and for the future Ormond would seek rather to contain than to overcome the Presbyterian refusal to conform.

32 *Cal. S.P. Ire., 1663–1665*, pp. 162, 174, 202.
33 Ibid., p. 324.

Exclusion, Conformity, and Parliamentary Representation: The Impact of the Sacramental Test on Irish Dissenting Politics

D. W. HAYTON

Various sensitive political issues were raised by the presence in early eighteenth-century Ireland of substantial numbers of Protestant dissenters, but the most persistently and vigorously debated was the propriety of maintaining the 'Test clause' imposed by the Irish Popery Act of 1704, which required all holders of civil and military office under the crown to receive Holy Communion in the established church. Such were the perceived effects, on employment opportunities for dissenters in central and local government, and on the composition of borough corporations, that very soon the Test came to be regarded by defenders and opponents alike as essential to the political ascendancy of the Church of Ireland interest. A die-hard churchman in the Irish House of Commons could declare 'that he would sooner part with his right hand'. For three decades or more, dissenting interests repeatedly sought the repeal of the Test, through appeals to public opinion, to their friends in the Irish Parliament, and to English government. But every time the issue was taken up by means of a parliamentary motion, dissenters suffered a humiliating defeat. Curiosity as to why such an apparently desperate quest should have been pursued for so long, through successive disappointments and rebuffs, forms a starting point for this paper. Why were dissenters so determined on repeal? What had they lost in 1704 that they thought might be regained? What had been the actual impact of the Test? It is these basic questions which need to be answered as precisely as possible before the wider significance of the Test as a political issue can begin to be explained.

Of course, churchmen in Ireland had been suspicious of, and hostile towards, Protestant dissenters ever since the Restoration, but the events of the Williamite Revolution and its aftermath added a new dimension to the 'dissenting question' in Irish politics, and focused attention on the problems created by the presence of a large and expanding Presbyterian population in Ulster. Fearful of the precedent set by Presbyterians' seizure of power in Scotland at the Revolution, Church of Ireland clerics viewed the consolidation in 1690 of the five Ulster Presbyteries into a General Synod as evidence of similar jurisdictional ambitions. Soon afterwards a new wave of Scottish immigration, driven by economic depression and agricultural failure, turned Anglican anxiety into near-paranoia: bishops and parsons thundered denunciations of the errors of Presbyterian theology, inadequacy of Presbyterian liturgy, and incapacity of Presbyterian orders. Some questioned Presbyterian loyalty to monarchy and constitution, recounting the past involvement of Scottish Covenanters and English Puritans in rebellion, republicanism, and regicide. Then, as Irish parliamentary struggles took on the form and rhetoric of English 'party' politics, the conflict between Church and Dissent became the very stuff of debate. In parliamentary speeches, as well as in sermons and pamphlets, Irish Tories condemned the Ulster Presbyterians, and Protestant dissenting communities in general, as enemies of the establishment.[1]

The situation in which dissenters found themselves at this time was peculiarly difficult. Not until 1719 did they enjoy even a limited measure of statutory toleration, and without legal protection they were technically liable to the full rigours of the Elizabethan and Restoration Acts of Uniformity. In practice the law requiring the entire population of Ireland to attend divine worship in the established church had proved unworkable, and dissenters absenting themselves from their parish church on Sunday were rarely prosecuted. However, there were other ways in which the law interfered with the exercise of their religion. From the mid-1690s efforts were made to prevent Ulster Presbyterian ministers from conducting marriages; church authorities exploited statutory powers to prevent the General Synod from setting up 'new' congregations; and, in a well-publicised episode, where freedom of conscience rather than freedom of worship was at stake, the Antrim grand jury presented, and enthusiastic magistrates imprisoned, three Presbyterian ministers who had refused to take the abjuration. Other grievances were also widespread: dissenters unable to send their children to be taught by those of their own persuasion; being obliged to bury their dead according to the order of service in the Church of Ireland; having to serve as churchwardens in their parishes; even being denied the opportunity to bid for leases on church or college land. And lurking in the background, even if infrequently articulated in the early eighteenth century, the frustration at having to pay a tithe to the parson as well as the pecuniary 'encouragement' expected by their own ministers.[2]

1   D.W. Hayton, 'Ireland and the English ministers, 1707–16', D.Phil dissertation, Oxford University, (1975), chapters 1, 5, 9–10; Raymond Gillespie, 'The Presbyterian revolution in Ulster, 1660–1690', in *The Churches, Ireland, and the Irish*, W.J. Sheils and Diana Wood (eds) (Oxford, 1989), pp 168–70; S.J. Connolly, *Religion, law, and power: the making of Protestant Ireland 1660–1760* (Oxford, 1992), pp. 79–80, 159–71; idem, 'Reformers and highflyers: the post-revolution Church', in *As by law established: the Church of Ireland since the Reformation*, Alan Ford, James McGuire, and Kenneth Milne (eds) (Dublin, 1995), pp. 152–65; Phil Kilroy, *Protestant dissent and controversy in Ireland 1660–1714* (Cork, 1994), chapters 7–8.
2   J.S. Reid, *History of the Presbyterian church in Ireland*, W.S. Killen (ed.) (3 vols., Belfast,

If there was no Toleration Act in Ireland in 1691, there was also no equivalent at that time of the English Test and Corporation Acts. Dissenters could take civil and military employments without hindrance, serve on the commission of the peace and other instruments of local government, hold office in borough corporations, and vote in parliamentary elections whatever the franchise. It soon became clear, however, that political participation was to be an issue in Ireland. High churchmen in England were already consoling themselves for what they saw as the deplorable effects of statutory religious toleration by cherishing the maintenance of the Anglican monopoly over public office, which, they argued, guaranteed the ultimate security of the establishment. As early as 1692 bishops of the Church of Ireland expressed a similar view. When it was proposed in the Irish House of Lords to adopt the English Toleration Act, episcopal votes pushed through a resolution calling for an extension to Ireland of the Test Act as well.[3] The same response was forthcoming three years later to a renewed proposal for toleration: 'I fear we shall be drowned with court holy water', wrote the Belfast Presbyterian minister, John McBride, 'as our act is not like to pass unless the Sacramental Test come along with it'.[4] What the vociferous clerical lobby eventually obtained was the best of both worlds: no toleration *and* the imposition of a Sacramental Test. In the winter of 1703/4 the continued exclusion of Protestant dissenters from governmental and municipal office was high on the political agenda in England, following the failure of a second bill at Westminster to outlaw 'occasional conformity'. The introduction of the first abortive bill to end this practice, in the autumn of 1702, had been interpreted by some Ulster Presbyterians as the harbinger of an Anglican clampdown on dissenting political interests in Ireland.[5] Now Tories on the English Privy Council, probably led by the earl of Nottingham, took the initiative, and inserted the 'Test clause' into an Irish Popery Bill, reasoning correctly that those in the Irish Parliament who called themselves Whigs would not reject a penal law, even at such a price.[6]

Almost immediately dissenting interests in Ireland began to lobby hard for the removal of the clause, but the Irish Parliament remained obdurate, even when the English and Irish governments interceded. In 1707 the English ministry made the first of several unsuccessful efforts to help: Lord Treasurer Godolphin, having changed the direction of Irish policy as a concession to the

1867), ii. 469–524; iii. 1–56; J.C. Beckett, *Protestant dissent in Ireland, 1687–1780* (London, 1948), chapters 3, 5–6, 11; Connolly, *Religion, law, and power*, pp. 162–4.

3   Cambridge University Library, Add. MS 1, f.104.
4   Sir J. Hamilton, *The Hamilton manuscripts* ..., T.K. Lowry (ed.) (Belfast, [1867]), p. 152.
    See also Bodleian Library, MS Ballard 8, f.70.
5   Trinity College Dublin [hereafter TCD], Lyons (King) collection, MS 1995–2008/962.
6   J.G. Simms, 'The making of a penal law (2 Anne, c. 6), 1703–4', *Irish Historical Studies* (1960–1), xii, 105–18.

Whig Junto, by appointing as viceroy a 'moderate' man, Lord Pembroke, sub-
mitted to a further proof of his good intentions by requesting Pembroke to
endeavour a repeal of the Test. The rapid rejection of the proposal, after a set-
piece debate in which two thirds of the Irish House of Commons voted against,
set the pattern for the future.[7] Two years later a Whig lord lieutenant, Lord
Wharton, schemed to secure repeal in the same way that the Test had been
introduced, by adding an appropriate clause in England to an Irish Popery Bill,
only to be foiled by his Cabinet colleagues, who forgot any promises and left his
draft bill untouched.[8] Not even the Whig triumphs at the Hanoverian succession brought relief. In 1716 a timorous Whig administration put forward a limited measure, to exempt only army and militia officers, but the strength of Irish
parliamentary feeling persuaded the English Privy Council to suppress it.[9] Another failure in 1719, when the duke of Bolton could obtain no more than a
restricted Toleration Act, and a short-term indemnity, ended agitation for a
time.[10] Then, in the early 1730s, when Presbyterian emigration from Ulster to
north America was causing grave concern, Sir Robert Walpole ordered his viceroy, the duke of Dorset, to try again. First an attempt modelled on Wharton's
plan, to add a repeal clause in England to a penal law originating in Ireland, was
dropped because of threats of opposition in the Irish Parliament; then a more
straightforward proposal to the Irish Commons was scuppered when the chief
'undertaker', Henry Boyle, who disliked the idea of repeal on principle, led a
managerial retreat from what he saw as a futile, and possibly counter-produc-
tive, gesture.[11]

Despite their many other grievances against the Church establishment, over
legal harassment, recognition of the validity of Presbyterian marriages, denial
of leases, and the exaction of tithe, dissenters concentrated their parliamentary

7   Hayton, 'Ireland and the English ministers', pp 178–9, 223–5; Reid, *History of the Pres-
    byterian church*, ii. 525–7; TCD, MS 1995–2008/1241; Historical Manuscripts Com-
    mission [hereafter HMC], *Ormonde MSS*, n.s. viii. 303–5; Leicestershire Record Office
    [hereafter LRO], Finch MSS, box 4950, bundle 22, Anderson Saunders to [Edward
    Southwell], 10 July 1707; BL, Add. MSS 9715, ff.163, 168, 170; 38155, ff.73–9.
8   D.W. Hayton, 'Divisions in the Whig Junto in 1709: some Irish evidence', *Bulletin of the
    Institute of Historical Research* (1982), lv, 206–14.
9   Reid, *History of the Presbyterian church*, iii. 66–79; Beckett, *Protestant dissent*, pp. 71–4.;
    Connolly, *Religion, law, and power*, p. 165; Christ Church, Oxford, Wake MSS, xii
    (unfoliated), Bp. Godwin of Kilmore to Abp. Wake of Canterbury, 27 February 1715/16,
    3 May, 9 June 1716.
10 Beckett, *Protestant dissent*, pp. 75–81; Connolly, *Religion, law, and power*, p. 165; Bodleian
    Library, MS Ballard 8, ff.55–6, 117–18; Christ Church, Wake MSS, xiii, items 71, 75,
    90; Public Record Office [herafter PRO], SP 63/377/135,137, 175, 226, 234–5.
11 Beckett, *Protestant dissent*, chapter 8; Connolly, *Religion, law, and power*, pp. 166, 169;
    HMC, *Egmont diary*, i, 450, 462–3; HMC, *Various collections*, vi. 57; Public Record Of-
    fice of Northern Ireland [hereafter PRONI], Shannon MSS, D2707/A1/2/89–90,
    Thomas Carter to Henry Boyle, 18 Jan. 1731/2, James Tynte to same, 5 Feb. 173[1/2];
    BL, Add. MS 21153, f. 12.

efforts on securing a repeal of the Test. As Bishop Godwin of Kilmore reported in 1717, 'nothing less will satisfy [them]'.[12] Statutory protection, through a Toleration Act, would certainly have offered a solution to some of their problems, but the prospect brought with it certain complications. The English act of 1689 had set a bad precedent, since it required subscription to articles of doctrine to which some Ulster Presbyterians might take objection. It was also felt to leave too much discretion to potentially unfriendly local magistrates. In 1692 the offer of a toleration to Irish dissenters at the price of the introduction of the Test had been 'rejected with scorn, and said to be "a giving them a stone instead of bread, and a serpent instead of fish" '.[13] The act of 1719, which in any case left important grievances unredressed, was very much a second best; not to be spurned of course, but not welcomed with any great acclamation. The immediate response of the General Synod of Ulster was to seek support in England for a possible repeal of the Test in the Westminster Parliament.[14]

In putting the case for repeal, dissenters were petitioning for the restoration of their 'civil rights' as loyal Protestants, but at the same time they took care not to give the impression that they were seeking political power. Considering the devotion they had shown to the Protestant establishment, to deny them 'the common rights of subjects', as the Presbyterian minister, John Abernethy, wrote in 1732, was 'unkind treatment ... so little deserved'; more insulting still, the plain political meaning was to 'rank them with papists'. But the most that Abernethy and other dissenting apologists claimed for their brethren was the right to 'perform service to the public', to assist in the defence of the state to which they had shown, and continued to show, such unwavering allegiance.[15] The worst effects of the Test, dissenting spokesmen observed, were felt in local government, where the absence of magistrates of their own persuasion hampered 'the free course of justice'; in other words, denied protection to ministers and congregations persecuted by high churchmen.[16] (They were less happy to claim that dissenters had been dissuaded from taking commissions in the militia, since this might lay them open to insinuations of disloyalty. Indeed, the extent to which nonconformists had, or had not, volunteered for militia service at times

---

12 Christ Church, Wake MSS, xii, Godwin to Wake, 13 April 1717.
13 *A representation of the present state of religion, with regard to infidelity, heresy, impiety, and popery* ... (Dublin, 1712), p. 13.
14 Bolton MSS (Lord Bolton, Bolton Hall, Wensley, Yorks.), D/73, Clotworthy Upton to [?John Barrington], 30 July 1719; PRONI, Rossmore MSS, T2929/2/48, Capt. John Henderson to Sir Alexander Cairnes, 31 October 1719.
15 John Abernethy, *The nature and consequences of the Sacramental Test considered* ... (Dublin, 1732), reprinted in John Abernethy, *Scarce and valuable tracts and sermons, occasionally published* (Dublin, 1751), pp. 84, 94, 104, 128. See also [James Kirkpatrick,] *An historical essay upon the loyalty of Presbyterians in Great-Britain and Ireland from the Reformation to this present year* ... ([Belfast], 1713), pp. 563–4.
16 BL, Add. MS 61640, ff.66–7.

of threatened Jacobite invasion, in 1708, 1715/16, and 1719, became a point at issue with their Anglican opponents.[17])

For tactical reasons, therefore, dissenters rarely demonstrated an enthusiasm to participate in politics, at borough or parliamentary level, but they could not wholly avoid the issue, for this was the favourite territory of high-church polemic. It was a stock argument of the various pamphlets and manuscript memorials in defence of the Test, which appeared or were reissued whenever the subject was raised in Parliament, that repeal would make no significant difference to the county magistracy, there being no more than a dozen JPs excluded by the enactment of the Test in 1704, and few dissenting landed proprietors with sufficient income to be candidates for reappointment.[18] Instead, from an Anglican point of view, the danger in relaxing the restriction on local office-holding was perceived to lie in the towns, especially the borough corporations of Ulster, where, according to polemicists like the fire-breathing vicar of Belfast, William Tisdall, self-serving cliques of Presbyterian merchants manipulated municipal and parliamentary elections in a sinister sectarian conspiracy to monopolise wealth and power to the detriment of honest churchmen.

Here was the real battleground on which the debate over the Test was fought. Tisdall and others of his kidney saw the activities of dissenting political interests in parliamentary boroughs, and the presence of dissenters in the Irish House of Commons, as a serious threat to the Church of Ireland ascendancy. It was this, more than anything else, that the Test had been introduced to forestall.[19] Dissenters themselves, though they steered clear of the issue in their own propaganda, were naturally sensitive to its importance. For nonconformist merchants individually, the dignity of civic office conferred a public recognition of their status, as well as a practical influence over urban affairs, which they might exert to their own advantage and to the benefit of their co-religionists. For the dissenting communities in general, unrestricted access to parliamentary representation was a guarantee that their voice would be heard by government, and thus that the many other grievances under which they laboured would be properly considered.

17 For example, William Tisdall, *A seasonable enquiry into that most dangerous political principle of the Kirk in power* ... (Dublin, 1713), pp. 24–6. According to one of the lords justices in 1715, Archbishop King, who as a former bishop of Derry was an old antagonist of the Ulster Presbyterians, only 42 nonconformists were put forward from the northern counties to take militia commissions in 1715, and several of those did not possess a substantial landed estate: TCD, MS 2533, pp. 133–4. See also TCD, MS 1995–2008/1723, Bp. Stearne of Dromore to Abp. King, 12 September 1715.

18 Tory or high church political interests seem repeatedly to have prepared, circulated, and argued from this kind of statistical evidence, whenever repeal of the Test appeared on the political agenda: see LRO, Finch MSS, box 4965, Ire. 9, 'The case of the sacramental test ...'; HMC, *Egmont diary*, i. 439.

19 William Tisdall, *The conduct of the dissenters of Ireland, with respect both to church and state* (Dublin, 1712), pp. 18–22, 34, 100.

In absolute terms the number of dissenters elected to the Irish House of Commons was always minuscule; a situation which could scarcely have improved without some radical reform of the electoral system. Not only was the dissenting population concentrated in the province of Ulster (dissenters in Dublin were a substantial but electorally ineffective minority); it was also excluded from meaningful political activity in all but a handful of parliamentary boroughs, most of which had been 'closed' by proprietorial interests. At no general election between 1692 and 1727 were more than nine dissenters returned to Parliament, out of an Irish House of Commons comprising three hundred Members. Interestingly, that peak was reached in 1703, the year before the imposition of the Test.[20] At the next election, in 1713, the total fell to five, at least in part as a result of determined efforts made by Tories and high churchmen within the Dublin administration against the return of Whiggish and dissenting candidates.[21] In the more favourable political climate of 1715 the number rose to seven or eight (one identification is uncertain),[22] but by 1727 it had dropped once more, to five or even four.[23]

Viewed as a proportion of the entire Commons membership, the decline would be statistically trivial; down from three per cent to no more than 1.3 per cent overall. There are, however, other ways of looking at the evidence, which would render it more significant. The first would be to calculate the number of dissenting MPs in 1727 as a proportion of the representation in 1703, which shows a rather more dramatic fall, of at least 55 per cent. Another would be to consider the types of constituency for which dissenters were elected. Invariably all were chosen in the province of Ulster, although in the case of Sir Alexander Cairnes, returned as knight of the shire for Monaghan in 1713 and 1715, the presence of a small minority of Presbyterian freeholders in his county, an area

20 Thomas Bell (Antrim), Edward Brice (Dungannon), William Cairnes (Belfast), William Craford or Crawford (Belfast), Hugh Hamill (Lifford), Sir Arthur Langford (Coleraine), James Lenox (Derry), Hans Stevenson (Killyleagh), and Clotworthy Upton (Co. Antrim). Identification of these and other dissenting MPs is based on my own researches, supplemented by the genealogical information presented in Jean H. Agnew, 'The merchant community of Belfast, 1660–1707' PhD dissertation, Queen's University, Belfast (1994), Appendices A-B.

21 Sir Alexander Cairnes (Co. Monaghan), Hugh Henry (Antrim), James Stevenson (Killyleagh), Clotworthy Upton (Co. Antrim), Thomas Upton (Antrim). On the 1713 election see J.G. Simms, 'The Irish Parliament of 1713', in *War and politics in Ireland, 1649–1730*, D.W. Hayton and Gerard O'Brien (eds) (London, 1986), pp. 278–81; D.W. Hayton, 'The crisis in Ireland and the disintegration of Queen Anne's last ministry', *Irish Historical Studies* (1980–1), xxii, 202–3.

22 Sir Alexander Cairnes (Co. Monaghan), Alexander Dalway (Carrickfergus), Archibald Edmonstone (Carrickfergus), Hugh Henry (Antrim), Sir Arthur Langford (Co. Antrim), James Stevenson (Randalstown), Clotworthy Upton (Co. Antrim), and possibly John McMullan (Antrim).

23 Sir Alexander Cairnes (Monaghan), Hugh Henry (Antrim), James Stevenson Sr (Killyleagh), James Stevenson Jr (Killyleagh), and possibly Thomas Upton (Derry).

on the frontier of the General Synod's jurisdiction, made little difference to the poll. More revealing is the proportion of Members returned for 'closed' boroughs, dependent solely on the favour of a patron or patrons, as opposed to the more 'open' constituencies, which were not dominated by proprietorial interest. For our purposes, county elections can be ignored, since the passage of the Test did not affect entitlement to the forty-shilling freehold franchise, and in any case Presbyterian voters were a force only in County Antrim, where the Uptons of Castle Upton held one seat from 1695 until 1713 and took both in 1715.[24] Two of the boroughs in which dissenters were successful in this period possessed a potwalloper franchise, Antrim town and Randalstown, and naturally deferred to proprietorial influence. Seven were corporation boroughs, but five of these were either pocket boroughs or were contested by rival patrons: Donegal town, Dungannon, Killyleagh, Lifford, and Limavady.[25] As 'open', or potentially 'open' constituencies, we can count only the more lively corporation boroughs of Belfast and Coleraine, where patronal influence might be challenged by the internal civic oligarchy; the single freeman borough in Ulster, Derry; and the county borough of Carrickfergus, whose two thousand strong electorate combined corporators, freemen, and freeholders: precisely the four constituencies upon which Tisdall focused his attention in the most vigorous of his contributions to the 'paper war' over the Test, *The conduct of the dissenters of Ireland, with respect both to church and state* (1712).[26]

Of the nine MPs returned in 1703, one represented County Antrim and only three sat for boroughs under the control of Presbyterian, or sympathetic Anglican, landlords. In 1713, after the imposition of the Test, no dissenting MP sat for an 'open' borough: two represented counties (Sir Alexander Cairnes in Monaghan and Clotworthy Upton in Antrim), with the other three nominated for 'closed' boroughs. The increase in numbers in 1715 brought, in addition to three county Members, two dissenters returned for Carrickfergus. But this was a short-lived reversal of a clear underlying trend, and after 1727 the quartet of unquestionably nonconformist Members all sat for pocket boroughs, including Cairnes, the former shire knight who now took refuge in the borough constituency of Monaghan town.

Thus it would seem that dissenting involvement in electoral politics did decline sharply in the three decades after the imposition of the Test, albeit from

---

24 William Tisdall, *The case of the Sacramental Test stated and argued* (Dublin, 1715), pp. 48–9, alleged that in the 1715 election in Co. Antrim Presbyterian freeholders were 'spirited up' by their 'teachers and elders' to resist their landlords' direction, 'however precarious their tenures were, or whatever obligations they lay under'.

25 The best guide to electoral interests in this period is the series of annotated lists of constituencies prepared for the Tory administration prior to the 1713 election, and preserved in the Southwell papers in the British Library: Add MS 34777, ff. 20–32, 42–4.

26 See above, n. 19.

a low base. By the 1730s the number of dissenters in the Irish House of Commons had fallen by more than half, and those who were able to scramble their way to a Commons seat owed their election either to their own proprietorial interest or to the recommendation of a sympathetic borough-monger. But how much of the decline was due directly to the Test? To answer this question involves looking more closely at the four 'open' (or potentially 'open') boroughs in Ulster, where, according to Tisdall, Presbyterian inhabitants, in particular the wealthy commercial elites, had, in varying degrees, exercised political influence before 1704: Belfast, Carrickfergus, Coleraine, and Derry. In the corporation boroughs, Belfast and Coleraine, the application of the Test would have a direct impact on parliamentary elections, in disqualifying voters; and a powerful impact too, since corporation electorates were so small. In the case of a borough with a wholly or partly freeman franchise, the effect would be indirect, though it might still prove decisive if it brought about a shift in the balance of power within the corporation, because the municipal authority could admit new freemen by grace, and thus flood the constituency with new, 'outlying', electors.

From the Williamite Revolution until 1704 these four boroughs had between them been able to guarantee a dissenting parliamentary presence at each general election. David Cairnes sat for Derry in 1692 and 1695, being joined in the second Williamite Parliament by Alderman James Lenox, while at the same time Sir Arthur Langford, of Summerhill, County Meath, captured a seat at Coleraine. In 1703 as many as four nonconformist Members were elected from the 'open' boroughs, with Lenox and Langford accompanied to the Commons by William Cairnes and William Craford, both of whom had been elected for Belfast. After 1703, on the other hand, the only dissenters chosen were Alexander Dalway and Archibald Edmonstone, for Carrickfergus in 1715, and both were unseated at the following general election, in 1727. A simple aggregate of the evidence would suggest a firm conclusion: that Presbyterians were driven off the commanding heights of municipal politics by the Test, and in these constituencies lost the capacity to return MPs of their own persuasion.

In each case, however, the detailed story was more complicated. Let us begin in Derry, where Presbyterians suffered their sharpest setback. By refusing to qualify themselves, no less than nine out of the twelve aldermen and fourteen out of the twenty-four burgesses forfeited their places on the common council, winning for themselves an imperishable glory, in so far as their names were inscribed on a commemorative tablet on the wall of the first Presbyterian church in the city, but effectively turning over the government of the borough to a Church of Ireland interest.[27] Within a fortnight of the mass resignation of

---

27 Reid, *History of the Presbyterian church*, ii. 511; Thomas Witherow, *Derry and Enniskillen in the year 1689* ... (Belfast, 1873), pp. 307–8.

the 'dissenting members of the corporation', a full court of aldermen had been reconstituted, and all but five of the vacant burgess-ships filled.[28] At the next parliamentary election the seat held by the disqualified Presbyterian alderman, James Lenox, went to a Tory army officer who had been admitted to the corporation in 1704, Colonel John Newton.

In a narrow sense this was indeed a defeat for Presbyterian political interests. It was the culmination of a power-struggle that seems to have been waged between the representatives of Church and Presbytery ever since the Jacobite siege of the city, when death and exile had reduced the common council to a mere four members, and opened the opportunity for a Presbyterian faction to take control of the corporation.[29] In the years that followed, vacancies in the court of aldermen were almost always supplied by Presbyterian burgesses, and new recruits to the burgess-ship almost always drawn from among the Presbyterian mercantile community, a fact which the aldermen did not dispute, although they denied any sectarian motive.[30] Encouraged by the local Church of Ireland establishment, especially Bishop William King (until his translation to the archbishopric of Dublin in 1703), the Anglican minority on the common council had made repeated efforts to turn back the tide, exploiting the influence their friends enjoyed in Dublin Castle. In 1691 and 1692 the Irish Privy Council disapproved the election to the mayoralty of a Presbyterian incumbent, on the grounds that it was illegal to 'hold over' in the office, but made no attempt to impose an Anglican alternative.[31] A similar situation arose in 1698, when two Presbyterian candidates were disapproved in succession, both of them recent appointments to the court of aldermen. This time the actions of the Privy Councillors were definitely prompted by religio-political motives, since they were responding to the protests of a rejected Anglican candidate for the mayoralty, Alderman Thomas Moncrieffe, who had complained of being repeatedly overlooked and had alleged a sectarian conspiracy to exclude all church-

28 TCD, MS 1995–2008/1106.
29 [Kirkpatrick], *An historical essay upon the loyalty of Presbyterians*, pp. 425–9; Sir Charles S. King, A *great archbishop of Dublin William King, D.D.* ... (London, 1906), p. 36. In 1718, referring to a ceremony in the city to commemorate the accession of George I Bishop Nicolson of Derry recorded that 'from the day that King James's forces were put to flight, to this present, the heart-burnings of parties prevailed so far that they could never be brought to an agreement in any common solemnity': Christ Church, Wake MSS, xii, Nicolson to [Archbishop Wake], 1 August 1718.
30 PRONI, LA79/28/2, Londonderry corporation minute book 1688–1704 (unfoliated), 12 January 1698.
31 [Kirkpatrick,] *An historical essay upon the loyalty of Presbyterians*, pp. 427–8; King, A *great archbishop of Dublin* ... p. 36; J.C. Beckett, 'William King's administration of the diocese of Derry, 1691–1703', *Irish Historical Studies* (1944–5), iv, 164–80; PRONI, LA79/28/2, 2 November 1691, 2 January 1691/2, 2, 29 November 1692; PRONI, Lenox-Conyngham MSS, T3161/1/3, William Conolly to James Lenox, 11 November 1693.

men from high municipal office.[32] Eventually the council was prevailed upon to accept a representative of one of the longer-established Presbyterian aldermanic families in what appears to have been a compromise settlement, and for several years Presbyterians and Anglicans alternated in the mayoralty. Moncreiffe continued to be kept out, and for their part Presbyterian officers agreed to behave with discretion, and not to parade the civic regalia at their own religious meetings.[33] In the winter of 1703/4 trouble flared up again. The common council's choice of a recently admitted Presbyterian alderman to succeed the outgoing mayor, Samuel Leeson, was ignored by the Irish Privy Council, presumably under the influence of the Tory lord lieutenant, Ormond. Without waiting for disapproval, councillors proceeded to a second election. This was explicitly disapproved, as was a third, until the Privy Council reversed its earlier judgements on the point of principle, and permitted the churchman Leeson to hold over.[34]

The dramatic events which followed the enactment of the Test can thus be viewed as bringing to an end more than a decade of conflict within the corporation, and forcing a victory for the church interest. But if we look more closely at the effects on parliamentary representation the picture changes. The Presbyterians in the city had in fact never attempted to reserve both parliamentary seats for their own brethren, being aware of the importance of having effective representation, and seeking to return Members whose voices would carry weight in the Irish House of Commons and with government. In the 1690s they had elected the Dutch merchant, Bartholomew Vanhomrigh, a revenue commissioner and the agent for Lord Athlone's Irish estates, together with their own burgess David Cairnes; and in 1703 the Presbyterian James Lenox had been joined as MP by an Anglican alderman, Charles Norman, even though Norman was Bishop King's most important friend (and frequent correspondent) in the corporation, and was one of the leaders of the faction that had promoted Moncreiffe's petitions.[35] Norman is also a significant figure in another respect, for, although a churchman, he was no high-flyer, and, indeed, voted with the Whig party in the Irish Parliament, which publicly espoused, even if it did not always effectively promote, the interests of Protestant dissenters.[36] It would be wrong to

32 *Reid, History of the Presbyterian church*, ii. 572; PRONI, LA79/28/2, 12 January, 2, 23 November 1698; PRONI, Lenox-Conyngham MSS, D1449/12/19, affidavit signed by George Squire and other aldermen and burgesses of Derry, 24 November 1698.

33 PRONI, LA79/28/2, 26 December 1698, 2 November 1699, 2 November 1700, 3, 29 November 1701, 2 November 1702; PRONI, T3161/1/6, Robert Rochfort to James Lenox, 6 Dec. 1701; TCD, MS 1995–2008/882, 983.

34 PRONI, LA79/28/2, 2, 23 November, 7, 21 December 1703.

35 TCD, MS 750(1), pp. 126, 130. For Vanhomrigh, see Wouter Troost, 'Letters from Bartholomew Van Homrigh to General Ginkel, earl of Athlone, 1692 to 1700 ...', *Analecta Hibernica* (1986), xxxiii, 61–4.

36 TCD, MS 1995–2008/983; 2531, pp. 14, 29; Hayton, 'Ireland and the English ministers', p. 335.

assume that the Anglican faction in the common council was necessarily Tory in its 'party' orientation. One of the new aldermen chosen in 1704 was William Conolly, a prominent Whig who in Parliament consistently supported the repeal of the Test. Conolly had acted as an adviser to, and agent for, the corporation of Derry during the political ascendancy of the Presbyterian interest, and continued in the corporation's employ long after 1704.[37] There were Tories to be found among the new corporators, of course. As early as 1707 the churchmen seem to have been divided among themselves over a mayoral election, with another petition to the Privy Council only averted by the timely intervention of Bishop (now Archbishop) King; and in the strained political atmosphere of 1713 the Tory John Newton was elected to Parliament alongside Charles Norman.[38] However, after the Hanoverian succession the Whigs recovered control, taking both seats in the general elections of 1715 and 1727, one of their successful candidates on the second occasion being Thomas Upton of Castle Upton, whose family had not long before been active in the Presbyterian cause, even if they were now in the process of conforming.

In Belfast corporation Presbyterians also made considerable political progress in the decade following the Revolution, and although by 1704 their position still fell some way short of the ascendancy enjoyed by their co-religionists in Derry, it was undoubtedly very strong. In her admirable study of the Belfast commercial elite in the later seventeenth century, Jean Agnew has calculated that as many as three quarters of the burgesses elected between 1689 and 1704 were Presbyterians. Just as in Derry, the early 1690s had marked a crucial stage in their advance, with the deaths of five conforming burgesses and their replacement by Presbyterians (all elected unanimously).[39] There was still no more than the narrowest majority, for of the fifteen burgesses who made up the corporation in 1704, only eight were nonconformists.[40] But the consistent support of two conforming burgesses, the brothers George and James Macartney, Whig Members for the borough in the 1692 Parliament, who belonged to an extended

---

37 See, e.g. PRONI, D1449/12/23, 31, 37–8, 41, 42, Conolly to John Harvey, 9 September 1699, 29 April 1701, 15 October 1703, same to John Deering, 12 November 1707, same to the mayor of Derry, 1 October 1709, same to Frederick Conyngham, 19 November 1709.
38 TCD, MS 2531, p. 14; Hayton, 'Ireland and the English ministers', p. 335.
39 Agnew, 'Merchant Community of Belfast', pp. 127–8.
40 The names of the burgesses, and the dates on which they were elected and replaced, are given in *The town book of the corporation of Belfast 1613–1816* ..., R.M. Young (ed) (Belfast, 1892), pp. 235–7. Presbyterians are identified in [Kirkpatrick,] *An historical essay upon the loyalty of Presbyterians*, p. 421. By the terms of the borough charter (ibid., p. 233) there should only have been thirteen (twelve *plus* the sovereign), but it is clear that the two constables of the castle, both Lord Donegall's appointees, were added to this number, possibly under some *ex officio* arrangement. The standard local history, George Benn, *A history of the town of Belfast* (1877) would in any case have been mistaken in stating that there were only twelve.

family with Presbyterian branches, made the margin more comfortable; and moreover the third earl of Donegall, the landed proprietor, showed no hostility to the recruitment of Presbyterian burgesses or to the repeated election of Presbyterians to the office of sovereign (chief magistrate) of the borough. Dr Agnew has claimed that eight out of the fourteen sovereigns elected between 1691 and 1704 were nonconformists, one of whom, the merchant David Butle, was in office at the time of the enactment of the Test clause.[41] The parliamentary representation had also come to reflect this Presbyterian predominance. In the 1695 election Donegall's brother, Hon. Charles Chichester, had been returned alongside George Macartney, but in 1703 the MPs chosen, presumably with Lord Donegall's blessing, were both local Presbyterian merchants, William Cairnes and William Craford.

Unlike their counterparts in Derry, the Presbyterian burgesses of Belfast did not resign en masse in 1704. In fact, they did not resign at all. To begin with, all that happened was that Butle stepped down as sovereign, to be replaced by George Macartney, who was then re-elected, with Presbyterian support.[42] And so things continued, for three years, with the Presbyterian burgesses as, so to speak, 'sleeping partners' in corporation affairs. The law was not evaded through 'occasional conformity'; it was ignored. There was some minor erosion of the nonconformist interest through natural selection. Two Presbyterian burgesses died, Captain David Smyth and Arthur Macartney (a half-brother of George and James), and in each case the replacement was a nominee of the Donegalls.[43] Hitherto this would not have been politically significant, but it would seem that, with the unexpected death of Lord Donegall in 1706, and the succession of his young son under the guardianship of the dowager countess, factional rivalry began to trouble the corporation. Whether, as some contemporaries believed, George Macartney took advantage of the Donegall minority to assert his own interest; or whether, in the gathering excitement of 'party' conflict in the Irish Parliament, the Chichesters and their allies were becoming more pronouncedly 'high church' and 'Tory' in their sympathies, is difficult to say.[44] Certainly, if Lady Donegall was anxious to promote a Tory interest, she chose an eccentric manner of doing so.

Open conflict broke out in 1707, at a parliamentary by-election necessitated by the death of William Cairnes, Lady Donegall and George Macartney each putting forward a candidate. Interestingly, both nominees were Presbyterians: Lady Donegall recommended Cairnes' brother, Sir Alexander, the wealthy

41 Agnew, 'Merchant community of Belfast', pp. 128–30.
42 *Town book of … Belfast*, ed. Young, pp. 194–5.
43 Ibid., pp. 235–7; Agnew, 'Merchant community of Belfast', pp. 132–4; Appendix, p. 47.
44 HMC, *Ormonde MSS*, n.s., viii. 312–13; Agnew, 'Merchant community of Belfast', pp 134–9; Peter Roebuck, 'The early years, 1737–64', in Peter Roebuck (ed.), *Macartney of Lisanoure, 1737–1806: essays in biography* (Belfast, 1983), pp. 4–5.

London financier who was later to sit as knight of the shire for Monaghan; Macartney an English nonconformist, Samuel Ogle. Admittedly, Sir Alexander Cairnes was a man of discretion, a political moderate who after 1710 was able to co-operate with the Tory administration of Lord Oxford, while Ogle made no secret of his sectarian affiliations: he often acted as a spokesman for nonconformity, and only a few years previously had been employed as an agent by the General Synod of Ulster to make representations to the English administration.[45] Perhaps confused by the presence of two candidates of their own persuasion, mindful of the dignity of property and the previous complacency of the Donegall family, and unwilling to draw attention to themselves, the Presbyterian burgesses did not vote. But one, Isaac Macartney, a connection of the sovereign's, made what seems to have been a tactical resignation of his burgessship to enable the choice of a replacement who would be able to appear conspicuously at the poll: John Haltridge, MP for Killyleagh, who was a conforming son of a Presbyterian minister. Haltridge's presence was to be vital, since three electors attended on each side. George Macartney then arrogated to himself a casting vote, as sovereign, and declared Ogle elected.[46]

From the point of view of the surviving Presbyterian burgesses, Macartney's electoral audacity proved fatal. Cairnes petitioned against the return, and although his arguments focused on the technical issue of whether the sovereign of a corporation could be allowed a second vote in the event of a tied contest, the presence of an unqualified burgess among his voters (ironically, not a dissenter) determined judgement against him. It also drew the attention of the House of Commons to the fact that the law was being flouted. The case had been heard in October 1707, just a few months after the Commons had rejected by a stunning majority Pembroke's cautious overtures towards a repeal of the Test. Members of Parliament resolved that the Belfast burgesses would have to do as the law required.[47] Despite being pressed to conform by Pembroke's ultra-Whig Chief Secretary, George Dodington, the rump of five Presbyterians, including Butle, Craford, and Edward Brice, who also sat in the House of Commons (for Dungannon), at last resigned their places.[48] As in Derry, occasional conformity does not seem to have been an option. When the Test clause was

45 For Cairnes, see HMC, *Portland MSS*, v. 259–60; for Ogle, ibid., iv. 82. Cairnes of course had a strong connection with Belfast, and he may have called upon to represent the interests of the town's Presbyterians a few years earlier in a dispute with William Tisdall: PRONI, D1449/13/1, letter book of David Butle, ff. 67–8, Butle to [Cairnes?], 6 November 1703.
46 Reid, *History of the Presbyterian church*, ii, 528–9; Agnew, 'Merchant Community of Belfast', pp 135–6; Appendix, p. 62; *The Journals of the House of Commons of the Kingdom of Ireland* (2nd edn, 23 vols, Dublin, 1763–86), iii. 521–2; HMC, *Ormonde MSS*, n.s. viii. 312–13; PRO, SP 63/366/252.
47 *Irish Commons' Journals*, iii. 521–2, 545–6; HMC, *Ormonde MSS*, n.s. viii. 312–13.
48 PRO, SP 63/366/252.

enforced, Presbyterian corporators excluded themselves, and gave way to church-men.

Once more, the impact of this debacle on parliamentary representation is not straightforward. The Donegalls certainly derived some benefit from the removal of the Presbyterian element from the corporation, and in succeeding general elections re-established their interest, but only as far as to be able to share the representation with the Macartneys. In 1713 the Earl's candidate, Anthony Atkinson, defeated a Presbyterian, James Stevenson, to secure the second seat behind Robert Moore. Circumstantial evidence indicates that Moore must have stood on a separate interest, presumably George Macartney's. For one thing Atkinson was a strong Tory and Moore, a younger son of the third Earl of Drogheda, a Whig; the Donegalls were expected to favour the high churchmen in this election, having cast aside their former even-handedness, while the Macartneys were described by the Tory administration's electoral spin doctors as 'v[ery] b[ad]'; and in 1715 John Chichester, the Donegall family candidate, was returned only after petitioning against Robert Moore's brother Capel.[49] This division of the spoils lasted beyond 1727, when the two Members elected were Hon. David John Barry, presumably on the Donegall interest, and George Macartney, jr, son and heir of the sovereign of 1707.[50] Whether the Chichesters were still clinging to the Toryism they had espoused in the latter stages of Queen Anne's reign is unclear, but the Macartneys would doubtless still have called themselves Whigs. Thus, if we take a long view, we find a similar outcome in Belfast to that in Derry: Presbyterians excluded from the corporation, and in consequence from the House of Commons, but Whig candidates, ostensibly sympathetic to nonconformist aspirations, continuing to hold at least one of the parliamentary seats.

Presbyterian corporators in Coleraine seem to have taken their cue from Derry rather than Belfast, leaving office in a body; at least, whether they had themselves resigned or been deprived, their replacements were all elected at one fell swoop in November 1704.[51] In fact, although the borough had returned a Presbyterian MP in 1695 and 1703, in the person of Sir Arthur Langford, the nonconforming interest in the corporation had been relatively slim: only two out of twelve aldermen and five out of twenty-four burgesses. Langford had presumably secured his return through the proprietorial influence of his nephew

49 BL, Add. MS 34777, ff. 26, 30, 42; *Irish Commons' Journals*, iii. 949, 954, 985; National Library of Ireland, MS 16007, pp. 28–30; Hayton, 'Ireland and the English Ministers', pp. 315, 334.

50 *Historical notices of old Belfast and its vicinity*, Robert M. Young (ed.) (Belfast, 1896), pp. 165–7, claims that the Donegall family had regained control of the borough by the mid-1720s.

51 PRONI, LA25/2AA/1A, Coleraine common council book 1672–1710, p. 227; T.H. Mullin, *Coleraine in by-gone centuries* (Belfast, 1976), p. 160.

and former ward, Hercules Rowley of Castleroe, and the backing of other important landed interests, in particular the Beresfords, who in political terms were effectively patrons of the borough.[52] Even though Sir Tristram Beresford, the then head of the family, had supported a churchman in the county by-election in 1697 against Alderman Lenox of Derry, there is no reason to suppose that he brought the same sectarian belligerence into borough politics.[53] From this premise, one would expect the events of 1704 in the corporation to have had little or no effect on parliamentary elections. Not so; the disqualifications which followed the Test opened the way for a rival interest to challenge the supremacy of the Beresfords. As in Belfast, where a minority in the Donegall family encouraged George Macartney to attempt a take-over, the succession of five-year-old Marcus Beresford on the death of his father Sir Tristram in 1701 created a power vacuum, which another local landowner, Captain William Jackson, was anxious to fill. The opportunity offered by seven vacancies (eight when one added in the failure of an elder Beresford to take the trouble to qualify himself) was quickly grasped. Jackson and his allies drafted in their own supporters and seized the mayoralty for one of their number, Arthur Cary, a coup which initiated a lengthy struggle for control between the Jacksons and the Beresfords.[54] In so far as Jackson and Cary seem to have espoused a fierce Toryism, the factional rivalry took on a partisan aspect which had some relevance to the political interests of dissenters, and the victories of the Beresford candidates at the general elections of 1713 and 1715 brought into the House of Commons two more Whig Members, one of whom, Lieutenant-General Frederick Hamilton of Walworth, had some national standing in the party. Again the figure of William Conolly, who had a local interest as the proprietor of the former Philips estate at Limavady, can be detected behind the scenes.[55]

Finally, we come to Carrickfergus, where a quite different situation prevailed. Here, without surviving assembly books for the period, it is impossible to say for certain whether any nonconformists were disqualified from among the seventeen aldermen and twenty-four burgesses who made up the corporation. Such evidence as we have, largely from selected transcripts of borough records made by later eighteenth-century antiquarians, suggests that no significant change occurred.[56] However, William Tisdall, whose acquaintance with

52 Mullin, *Coleraine in by-gone centuries*, pp. 137–9. Compare the reality with the alarmist exaggeration in Tisdall, *Conduct of the dissenters*, p. 19.
53 PRONI, T3161/1/4, poll for Co. Londonderry, 22–26 Apr. 1697.
54 Mullin, *Coleraine in by-gone centuries*, chapter 10. See also PRONI, T974/2, transcripts from Irish Privy Council records (since lost) regarding the election of magistrates for Coleraine.
55 TCD, MS 1995–2008/1284, 1572, 1622; Hayton, 'Ireland and the English ministers', p. 328.
56 Samuel M'Skimin, *The history and antiquities of the county of the town of Carrickfergus, from the earliest records, to the present time* (Belfast, 1811); PRONI, T2707, extracts by

the affairs of Carrickfergus extended to the ownership of property there, claimed in his *Conduct of the dissenters* that by 1712 the borough had come to be dominated by a quartet of occasionally conforming or outright nonconforming aldermen, supported by a 'vast' Presbyterian majority among the freemen, including a host of 'outlyers' from Belfast imported for the purpose.[57] In this instance, there is at least some circumstantial evidence to suggest a connection between Tisdall's conspiracy theory and political reality. Evidently municipal and parliamentary elections in Carrickfergus were being contested between two factions: one headed by Alderman Samuel Davys, who was enough of a loyal Anglican to bestow a gift of plate and other benefactions on his parish church in 1714,[58] and whose party loyalties were clearly Tory; and a more Whiggish interest headed by Alderman Edward Clements. In 1711 Davys protested to the Privy Council against Clements' re-election as mayor. His petition, and Clements' response, make it clear that the Whig faction included four aldermen, as Tisdall had reported, and two-thirds of the freemen.[59] Aided by Tories in the government, Davys secured the mayoralty for himself in 1712 and 1713, and two of his own family were returned as MPs in the 1713 general election. Both voted with the Tories in the Commons.[60] By 1715, with George I on the throne and a Whig administration in Dublin Castle, Clements had resumed sway, and two Whig MPs were elected. Significantly, they were not only local men; they were also Presbyterians. But this cannot necessarily be taken to clinch the argument for believing Tisdall's allegations: for one thing, neither of the new Members, Dalway and Edmonstone, appear to have been members of the corporation, even though they were local men; for another, it would be strange if Presbyterians in Carrickfergus should have been able to retain their places where those in Belfast could not, or, alone among Ulster dissenters, should have been prepared to conform occasionally to preserve their civic dignity. It would seem more reasonable to describe the Clements faction as sympathetic to Presbyterianism rather than as Presbyterian itself, or even crypto-Presbyte-

Dean Richard Dobbs of Carrickfergus borough records, 1785. The calendar to these documents takes the form of a complete typescript copy of the original volume. On p. 162 there is a list of aldermen and burgesses in 1681, to which further names are then added, without accompanying dates. I was able to make a search through the surviving original borough records by kind permission of Carrickfergus Borough Council. Thanks are due to Mrs Helen Rankin for her good offices in this matter.

57 Tisdall, *Conduct of the dissenters*, pp. 21–2. Details of his Carrickfergus property are to be found in Carrickfergus borough records, vol. ix, p. 24. There was of course a strong Presbyterian element in the resident population of the town: see the comments of the Duke of Schomberg in 1690 (*Calendar of state papers, domestic, 1689–90*, p. 220).

58 M'Skimin, *History and antiquities of ... Carrickfergus*, p. 48.

59 Marsh's Library, Dublin, MS Z.3.2.6/28. See also PRONI, T2707, calendar, pp. 173–4.

60 M'Skimin, *History and antiquities of ... Carrickfergus*, p. 166; ibid., E.J. M'Crum (ed) (2nd edn, Belfast, 1909), p. 473; Hayton, 'Ireland and the English ministers', p. 323.

rian; in other words, a Whig interest like those in Derry, Belfast and Coleraine. What made Carrickfergus different was that, while the other 'open' boroughs all returned churchmen after 1704, the partly Presbyterian electorate that Clements and his fellow Whigs in the assembly had helped to create enabled a successful Presbyterian candidacy in 1715. This was a short-lived triumph, however, as over the next twenty years more powerful proprietorial interests asserted themselves in the borough, and intruded non-resident freemen of a rather different complexion; above all Lord Conway, the governor of the castle, whose protégé Arthur Dobbs was chosen in 1727 in a more characteristic eighteenth-century election, at a cost of some £1000.[61]

The general conclusion to these detailed studies must be that only in Derry and Belfast did the imposition of the Test have a direct effect on Presbyterian parliamentary representation. Sir Arthur Langford's seat for Coleraine had not been obtained through the efforts of a sectarian interest in the corporation; while the election of two Presbyterian Members for Carrickfergus in 1715 was, if anything, a by-product of the conflict between party factions. By themselves, the two other borough constituencies, where indigenous Presbyterian interests were a powerful force before 1704, had only accounted for the return of a single dissenting MP in 1692 and in 1695, and three in 1703. One lesson might be that if we are to search for the reasons for the long-term decline in the number of nonconformists returned to Parliament after 1704 we must look elsewhere in Ulster, to the 'closed' boroughs and counties, where what mattered was the influence of individual landlords. It was indeed precisely in this area that the most damaging blows were delivered to the dissenting political interest in the early eighteenth century, in a decisive fall in the number of Presbyterian proprietors able to stand on their own interest for knight of the shire, to nominate to their own pocket boroughs, or to persuade electoral patrons to recommend them elsewhere.

In the first three decades of the eighteenth century the Presbyterian element within the Ulster landed elite underwent a progressive and seemingly inevitable decline. In about 1720 the compiler of a list of the 'gentlemen' of County Antrim, defined as those possessing incomes from landed property of at least £100 a year, found less than twenty dissenters and three times that many Anglicans, of whom eight were noted to be the sons of dissenters.[62] In another similar exercise, this time covering the entire province of Ulster, and seeming

61 M'Skimin, *History and antiquities of ... Carrickfergus* (1811), pp. 78, 166; (1909), p. 462; Carrickfergus borough records, vol. ix, p. 3, memorial to lords justices and Privy Council, 27 June 1732; Desmond Clarke, *Arthur Dobbs Esquire 1689–1765 ...* (Chapel Hill, N. Carolina, 1957), pp. 24–5.
62 Royal Irish Academy, MS 24.K.19/1. See also Toby C. Barnard, 'Identities, ethnicity and tradition among Irish dissenters *c.*1650–1750', in K. Herlihy (ed.), *The Irish dissenting tradition* (Dublin, 1995), pp. 34–5.

from internal evidence to have been drawn up about a decade later, almost certainly as part of a propaganda campaign against a repeal of the Test, the number of dissenters was given as only eight, one of whom had a 'Churchman' as his heir.[63] According to this second list, the proportion of churchmen to Presbyterians within the nine counties was now over twelve to one. What is more, the further outlook for nonconformity appeared gratifyingly bleak: 'in this list of dissenters, there are several whose apparent heirs are churchmen, but not one churchman whose apparent heir is a dissenter, so that in a few years, in all likelihood, the disproportion will greatly increase, it having been observed that a great many dissenters of considerable estates have of late years come over to the Church'.

Presbyterian writers who countered such analyses with more optimistic figures of their own seem to have been whistling in the wind.[64] Presbyterian gentlemen were a visibly diminishing presence not only at elections and in Parliament, but in the meetings of the General Synod of Ulster, where after 1715 the number of lay elders attending began to decrease, and, more to the point, substantial landed proprietors occupying positions of responsibility were fewer and further between. It had not always been so. In 1706 the synod had been able to institute a scheme to encourage donations from 'public spirited gentlemen of our persuasion' to finance the setting up of new congregations, appointing twenty-two such 'gentlemen' from the nine presbyteries to promote the subscription, including six present or future MPs.[65] But no similar appeal to the landed interest can be traced subsequently, as the number of Presbyterian squires dwindled. By the 1730s even the new squire of Castle Upton was a Churchman. John Upton had succeeded his brother Clotworthy, who for many years had been the most visible Presbyterian landlord in Ulster, the only one with enough influence to challenge consistently, and successfully, for a county seat in Parliament, and the only dissenting gentleman appointed as deputy governor of a county in 1714. Clotworthy Upton's death in 1725 would have been a major setback to the Presbyterian cause without the additional misfortune of his successor being an Anglican, however well-intentioned the new squire professed himself to be.[66]

The importance of the Test in initiating or accelerating the trend towards conformity can only be surmised. The absence of attested examples of 'occa-

63 Lambeth Palace Library, MS 1742, ff. 49–56.
64 John Abernethy, in *Reasons for the repeal of the Sacramental Test* (Dublin, 1733), repr. in Abernethy, *Scarce and valuable tracts and sermons*, p. 61, claimed that in three counties of Ulster 'there are above sixty dissenting gentlemen, who possess estates from £200 per annum to £1400'.
65 *Records of the General Synod of Ulster from 1691 to 1820* (3 vols, Belfast, 1890–8), i. 115–16.
66 PRO, SP 63/371/66; Thomas Witherow, *Historical and literary memorials of Presbyterianism in Ireland (1623–1731)* (London, 1879), pp. 207–8.

sional conformity' might be taken to suggest that few propertied dissenters responded pragmatically to the requirements of the law, though on the other side one could point to a number of conforming Presbyterian proprietors who maintained links with their past life. We have seen, for example, how John Haltridge of Dromore, the conforming son of a Scottish Presbyterian merchant, and the nephew of two Presbyterian ministers, was brought in as a burgess of Belfast in 1707 to replace Isaac Macartney and vote in the parliamentary by-election in which most nonconformist burgesses abstained. The Rosses of Rostrevor, County Down, may have been another outwardly conforming family still identifying at local level with the interests of their Presbyterian tenantry.[67] What can be argued, however, is that even the most tentative of conformists seem ultimately to have progressed from pragmatism to conviction; and within a few generations to a full identification with the established church. Historians have still to investigate whether this phenomenon was confined to the landed elite, or extended to those prosperous commercial dynasties, especially in Belfast, for whom the enforcement of the Test clause meant the wrecking of civic ambitions. Clearly conformity was not induced immediately among the merchant aldermen and burgesses of Derry or Belfast, but in the long term the descendants of the martyrs of 1704 and 1707 may have been able to relocate themselves within the establishment.

Besides raising the issue of conformity, and its long-term significance, an examination of the history of dissenting parliamentary representation also points up the heightened importance after 1704 of what we might call in this context the 'virtual representation' of dissenters; that is to say the legislative and political assistance which might be afforded them by sympathetic churchmen, or, in an anachronistic terminology, 'liberal Anglicans'. These 'virtual representatives' would include the Whigs returned for counties and boroughs in Ulster which previously had elected Presbyterian Members: men like Charles Norman in Derry, the Macartneys in Belfast, General Frederick Hamilton in Coleraine. At their head, as we have already seen, was William Conolly, one of the great political manipulators of the period, whose informal electoral empire took in not only these more 'open' boroughs but also a raft of smaller, 'closed' constituencies, in counties Londonderry and Donegal, and whose 'Ultonian' connection helped propel him to the forefront of early Hanoverian parliamentary management. As Speaker of the Irish House of Commons after 1715 Conolly seems to have taken upon himself the role of parliamentary patron of the dissenting cause, and to have made not only promises about repeal of the Test in 1716 and 1719, but even some attempt to fulfil them.[68]

67　Lambeth Palace Library, MS 1742, fo. 50; John Stevenson, *Two centuries of life in Down* (Belfast, 1920), pp. 149–51.
68　BL, Add. MS 61640, ff. 95–6; PRO, SP 623/377/167, 235; Bolton MSS, D/73, Clotworthy Upton to [?John Barrington], 30 July 1719.

In retrospect the limits of liberal Anglicanism in this period are plain to see, but the eyes of early eighteenth-century Presbyterians were covered with a film of optimism, engendered by the nature of political divisions in Ireland in the reign of Queen Anne. The opposition of Whigs to Tories hinged on a fundamentally different approach to religious policy and the defence of the Protestant establishment: Whigs proclaimed the need to create unity among Protestants, conformists and nonconformists, in order to withstand the expected onslaught of the Jacobites. While the 'rage of party' persisted, the repeated failure of Whig MPs to match words with deeds did not seem to matter: party rhetoric, on both sides, reinforced the image of the Whigs as defenders of nonconformist interests. It was easier to believe Whig excuses if the alternative was so much worse. But once the Tories had apparently been defeated for good, Protestant dissenters expected that they would share in the victory of the 'honest party'. Pressing their case to the incoming George I, Presbyterians recalled how they had not opposed the Test at its introduction, 'by themselves or their friends in the House [of Commons], by a promise made [by] several leading Members that they would take the first occasion that offered to repeal that clause, and this promise the Protestant dissenters think they have good reason to expect the performance of'.[69] It was the dashing of their hopes by a predominantly Whig House of Commons—in 1716, in 1719, in 1731/2 and in 1733—that seems finally to have convinced Presbyterians of the inadequacy of their 'virtual representation', on this issue and more generally. In 1719 Clotworthy Upton made all kinds of excuses to explain the hostility of elements within the Court party who might have been expected to support repeal - pique, ambition, the influence of 'great men'—but was obliged to admit that many had acted 'from principle'. Writing to a correspondent in England he belatedly echoed a comment made by Pembroke's chief secretary a dozen years before, that 'the generality of the gentlemen of this country', although 'state Whigs', were 'bigoted Church Tories', a vein of sentiment to be found even among some of Speaker Conolly's 'Ultonians'.[70] When a Whig like Henry Maxwell of Finnebrogue, County Down, a political client who followed Conolly so closely that he was popularly known as 'the Speaker's echo', reaffirmed his own personal commitment to the retention of the Test at the very same time that his patron was 'appearing openly' for repeal, the conclusion was inescapable, that even if the goodwill of a man like Conolly might be relied upon, his capacity to help was limited.[71]

If we wish to weigh the real effects of the Test clause on the political interest

---

69 BL, Add. MS 61640, ff.66–7.
70 PRO, SP 63/366, ff. 87–8; Bolton MSS, D/73.
71 BL, Add. 9715, f. 174; BL, Add. MS 61640, fos. 95–6; Surrey RO (Guildford), Midleton MSS, 1248/3 f. 386. For Maxwell, see Caroline Robbins, *The Eighteenth-century commonwealthman* (Cambridge, Mass., 1959), pp. 6, 147–9, 416–17. He was a brother-in-law of the Presbyterian MP Edward Brice, but was descended from clerical stock, and

of Protestant Dissent in Ireland, we must look beyond those borough corporations from which nonconforming aldermen and burgesses were so publicly excluded after 1704. Only in Derry and Belfast did this process of group disfran-
chisement make a difference to the balance of electoral power. Instead, the Ulster Presbyterian community lost much of its already meagre resources of direct parliamentary representation as a result of the creeping spread of conformity among the landed, and to a lesser extent the mercantile, classes who
provided the parliamentary candidates, and the effective electorate in pocket
boroughs. The loss of direct representation could have been offset to some degree by the 'virtual representation' provided by supposedly sympathetic churchmen, ostensibly Whiggish in their politics, a significant number of whom were
followers of Speaker Conolly in the reign of George I. But the repeated failure
of 'liberal Anglicanism' in general, and Conolly's Court party in particular, ad-
equately to support dissenters' interests in the Irish Parliament, served to em-
phasise, and indeed to magnify, the damage the Test had wrought.

stock, and in a debate in the Irish House of Commons in 1703, when he argued
strongly against the maintenance of the *regium donum*, declared himself to be 'alway[s]
a Churchman': D.W. Hayton, 'A debate in the Irish House of Commons in 1703: A
whiff of Tory grapeshot', *Parliamentary History*, x (1991), 161. See also TCD, MS
750(5), pp. 179–80, Abp. King to Lord Southwell, 16 July 1719, describing the defeat
of repeal as follows: 'The most zealous Whigs, and even those under distress of the
government, exerted themselves on this occasion and declared themselves with warmth
for preservation of the constitution in church and state, and particularly in relation to
the Test.'

For advice on various problems connected with the production of this essay, I am indebted
to Jean Agnew, Toby Barnard, Eoin Magennis, Ian Montgomery, and Rosemary Richey. For
permission to use, and to quote from, manuscript material, I must also thank His Grace the
archbishop of Armagh; the Lord Bolton; the Lord Rossmore; the earl of Shannon; the British Library Board; the Keeper of Western Manuscripts, Bodleian Library; the Governing
Body of Christ Church, Oxford; the National Trust; the Director, Public Record Office of
Northern Ireland; and the Board of Trinity College Dublin.

1780 Revisited: The Politics of the Repeal of the Sacramental Test

JAMES KELLY

Among the amplitude of landmark constitutional, commercial and civil statutes ratified by the Irish parliament in the late 1770s and early 1780s, the repeal of the requirement that Presbyterians who aspired to civil and military office should receive the eucharist 'according to the usage of the Church of Ireland'—the Sacramental Test—is generally accorded only passing mention. This may be because it generated only a fraction of the passion the legislation to relieve Catholics excited and did not, in practical terms, significantly enhance the position of Presbyterians. At the same time, the history of the repeal of the Test is of more than passing significance in the history of Irish dissent. Perhaps appropriately, given the way in which the Test was introduced, the campaign to secure its repeal arose out of an attempt in 1778 to revoke a number of penal laws against Catholics. However, the manner of its abolition differs markedly from the repeal of the penal laws. Whereas the cause of Catholic relief was dextrously represented by the Catholic Committee,[1] Presbyterians did not possess a comparable body to advance their claims. More consequently, because ministers could identify no compelling political or military reason why they should dilute the legal disabilities against dissenters the attempt to secure the abolition of the Test in tandem with Catholic relief failed in 1778. This greatly disappointed the small number of MPs who pressed the issue then, but the incongruity of the empowerment of Catholics while Presbyterians were left unrelieved was too much for Irish MPs to bear, and they were able to take advantage of the decline in governmental authority in Ireland to ensure that a relief bill was approved during the 1779–80 session with little public fuss. However, behind the scenes powerful vested political and religious interests maintained their opposition to the measure, and their actions are as central to the story of the repeal of the Test as the doggedness of Sir Edward Newenham, who deserves most of the credit for securing its final revocation.

1   Thomas Bartlett, *The fall and rise of the Irish nation: the Catholic question 1690–1830* (Dublin, 1992), pp. 86–91; R.E.Burns, 'The Catholic relief act in Ireland, 1778' in *Church History* (1963), xxiv, pp. 181–206; R.Kent Donovan, 'The military origins of the Roman Catholic relief programme of 1778', *Historical Journal* (1985), xxviii, pp. 79–102.

I

Though internal civil and religious divisions contributed to the failure of Presbyterians to advance their claim for full civil rights in the mid-eighteenth century,[2] they were less consequential than the continuing prejudices of powerful sections of the Anglican establishment towards those whom Mary Delany described in 1752 as 'querulous people'. Mrs Delany's uncharacteristically catty remark is attributable to her clerical husband's difficulties with Presbyterians in his County Down living, but her readiness to employ this and other equally unflattering designations reflects a disposition widely indulged by those securely nested in the Church of Ireland elite.[3] Many were even more antagonistic. One of the compilers of the 1766 religious census in the diocese of Armagh labelled Presbyterians as the 'avowed enemies to all civil and religious establishments' and accused them of 'the most violent and furious persecution of the established clergy' during 'the rebellious insurrection' staged by the Hearts of Oak agrarian movement a few years previously.[4] Such animus must have been borne out of personal experience, because while it was commonplace for members of the Church of Ireland to bemoan the anti-episcopal views of Presbyterians, to lament the danger caused to the Protestant community at large by 'division' within their ranks and to urge Presbyterians to join the Church of Ireland, most avoided abuse.[5] Indeed, some Whigs and Patriots were well-disposed, believing that

> the Presbyterians in *Ireland*, by their conduct now and at the time of the Rebellion, have ... shewn the most unshaken loyalty to his majesty and the most steady adherence to the liberty and property of the people.[6]

It is difficult to assess how prevalent this view was in Irish Protestant society. The fact that Charles Lucas' supporters chose Thomas Read, a 'new light' Presbyterian, as their candidate following Lucas' flight in 1749 might suggest

2 J.C. Beckett, *Protestant dissent in Ireland 1688–1780* (London, 1949); Peter Brooke, *Ulster Presbyterianism* (Dublin, 1987); J.S. Reid, *History of the Presbyterian Church* (3 vols, Belfast, 1867), ii, passim.

3 Lady Llanover, (ed.), *Autobiography and correspondence of Mary Granville, Mrs Delany* (6 vols, London, 1861–2), iii, pp. 71, 75.

4 Tomás Ó Fiaich, 'The 1766 religious census', *Seanchas Ardmhacha* (1960–61), iv, p. 158.

5 Historical Manuscripts Commission [hereafter HMC], *Reports on manuscripts in various collections, Knox papers* (London, 1909), vi, p. 68; J.G. McCoy, 'Court ideology in mid-eighteenth century Ireland', M.A. thesis, St Patrick's College Maynooth, 1990, p. 49–50.

6 *Patriot queries occasioned by a late libel, entitled queries to the people of Ireland* (Dublin, 1753), no 103.

that it was shared by many, but the ability of his opponents to embarrass him politically by alleging he was sympathetic to dissent suggests that those who held cordial attitudes toward dissenters were a minority located at the liberal end of the Whig-Patriot spectrum.[7]

Despite this, there was a definable Presbyterian interest in the mid-eighteenth century in those constituencies in Dublin and Ulster which had a sizeable Presbyterian population. Its influence in Dublin city derived from the estimated 17 per cent of the freemen who were Presbyterian, and its weight is attested to by the presence of Presbyterians on the board of aldermen.[8] The precise impact of this electoral interest on the character of Dublin politics remains opaque. But there is reason to believe that the support dissenters showed for Charles Lucas' campaign for municipal reform in the 1740s translated into support for the Patriot cause in the 1750s, for the campaign for legislation to limit the duration of parliaments to seven years in the 1760s and for the agitation in the early 1770s to give effect to the principle that 'the people, in a political sense, must ever be considered as our sovereign Lord, or king over all'. To this end, an attempt was made in 1774 to institute an arrangement whereby members of parliament consulted with their constituents and undertook to advance policies aimed at making parliament more representative and less venal.[9] The repeal of the Sacramental Test and other Presbyterian grievances did not figure specifically on this agenda. However, members of the Dublin Society of Free Citizens and the Aldermen of Skinner's Alley who were committed to reform recognized that Presbyterians had a legitimate grievance. Their electoral impact was less than overwhelming, but the fact that Sir Edward Newenham was returned to represent the constituency of County Dublin in the 1776 general election, that Napper Tandy was nominated to serve on the Common Council of Dublin Corporation in 1777, and that the Presbyterian merchant Travers Hartley was elected to represent the city in 1782 attests to the existence of an increasingly active popular interest that was well-disposed towards dissent in the capital.[10]

Compared with Dublin, Ulster politics were largely uneventful in the mid-eighteenth century. Indeed, Ulster Presbyterians were discreet to the point of political invisibility during the 1760s and early 1770s. However, there were signs in the mid-1770s that Presbyterian voters were disinclined to remain passive

7   See, generally, Sean Murphy, 'The Lucas affair', MA dissertation, University College Dublin (1981), passim.

8   J.R.Hill, 'Dublin corporation, Protestant dissent, and politics, 1660-1800' above; Murphy, 'The Lucas affair', p. 37; Ian McBride, 'Presbyterianism in the penal era', *Bullán* (1994), i, p. 82.

9   James Kelly, 'Parliamentary reform in Irish politics 1760-90' in David Dickson, et al., eds., *The United Irishmen* (Dublin, 1993), pp. 75-6.

10 *Ibid.*, pp. 76-7; E.A.Coyle, 'Sir Edward Newenham—the 18th Century Dublin Radical' in *Dublin Historical Record* (1993), xlvi, pp. 17, 21.

any longer. The most striking evidence of this is provided by their opposition to the controversial 1774 enactment excluding dissenters from voting in vestries. This did not result in the emergence of what one can define as an organized movement, but throughout the province Presbyterians assembled to prepare petitions (thirty-nine in all) against the measure, and in counties Londonderry and Antrim independent candidates were encouraged to stand against local establishment interests. The independent candidate in Londonderry withdrew before the election took place, but in County Antrim, dissatisfaction with the sponsorship by John O'Neill of the vestry voting provision was so sharp that an 'association' was established to advance the candidacy of Captain James Wilson who undertook to be guided in his actions by the wishes of his constituents. Wilson did not commit himself publicly to pursue the repeal of the Sacramental Test or any other Presbyterian grievance, but it is clear that it was the Presbyterian vote that ensured his election in 1776.[11] His return, when taken in tandem with Sir Edward Newenham's success in County Dublin, has been interpreted accurately as a victory for the cause of parliamentary reform rather than the cause of Presbyterian relief, but the fact that it was deemed expedient to annul the vestry voting provision in 1776 was a warning to all MPs in constituencies with Presbyterian voters to be more alert to their interests and concerns.[12] The absence of an effective Presbyterian organization freed them from the necessity of taking a public stand on the Sacramental Test. But, it is fair to say that by the late 1770s circumstances were potentially more favourable to Irish Presbyterians securing relief than they had been at any point in several decades.

If the electoral and political factors just described provide one reason for this, the easing in denominational hostility on the ground, observed by the respected Church of Ireland divine Philip Skelton, provides another.[13] However, since nobody was actively agitating the cause of Presbyterian relief, it did not seem likely in the near future until the suggestion in 1778 that some of the penal laws against Catholics should be repealed galvanized an uneasy coalition of anti-Catholic and pro-dissenter interests to take up the cause.

11 Ibid., p 77; *Hibernian Journal*, 30 May, 1 July 1774, 17 May 1775; W.H. Crawford and Brian Trainor, (eds), *Aspects of Irish social history* (Belfast, 1969), nos 69 and 70; R.B.McDowell, *Ireland in the age of imperialism and revolution 1760–1801* (Oxford, 1979), pp. 294, 296.

12 *Hibernian Journal*, 1 July 1774; *Finn's Leinster Journal*, 25 June 1774, 1 November 1775.

13 HMC, *Knox papers*, pp. 443–4.

II

Though there were an exceptional number of critical political, military and commercial matters to occupy the minds of MPs during the 1777–8 session, the
issue which excited greatest passion was the proposal to enhance Catholic civil
rights. Because of the extensive behind-the-scenes preparations this legislation
necessitated, both its proponents and opponents had plenty of time to prepare
their positions prior to Luke Gardiner's request to the House of Commons on
25 May 1778 for permission to introduce heads of a bill for Catholic relief.[14]
Gardiner's request was received positively by a convincing majority of those
present, though 'the leading parliamentary spokesmen for the Protestant dissenters', Hercules Langford Rowley, was among those who urged caution. Rowley
did not make any explicit allusion to the disabilities under which Presbyterians
operated in the course of his statement, but it was implicit in his call for 'the
liberty of mankind in general' and his recommendation that nothing should be
done that would weaken the Protestant interest.[15] Sir Edward Newenham was
characteristically more forthright. As soon as Gardiner was given the authorisa-
tion he sought, he requested leave to bring in the heads of a separate bill for the
relief of 'Protestant dissenters', and authorization was given *nemine contradicente*
for Boyle Roche, the MP for Tralee, and he to prepare an appropriate bill.[16]

The brevity of the surviving reports indicate that Newenham offered little
by way of explanation of his motion or his motives on 25 May. On the face of it,
he was simply taking advantage of the moment to ensure that Presbyterians
were not disadvantaged *vis à vis* Catholics. However, if this was his priority, his
anti-Catholic proclivities (so visible when he was High Sheriff for Dublin County
in the 1760s) suggested that he was not neutral on the subject of Catholic relief,
though he was careful to reserve his opinions while he awaited directions from
'the gentlemen, clergy and freeholders of the County of Dublin'.[17]

Despite Newenham's reputation, the proponents of Catholic relief were not
disquieted by his blatant attempt to advance the cause of Presbyterian relief by
linking it to their cause. Indeed, Hervey, the Earl-Bishop of Derry, expressed
the opinion of many supporters of Gardiner's bill, when he recommended that
the grievances of both interests should be ameliorated on the grounds that 'a
seasonal indulgence to the Presbyterian and Papist may save the kingdom'.

14 Described in Burns, 'Catholic relief', pp. 183–9.
15 Burns, 'Catholic relief', pp. 191–2; *Journal of the House of Commons on the kingdom of
    Ireland* (19 vols, Dublin, 1796–1800), ix, 475.
16 Sir Henry Cavendish's parliamentary diary 1776–89 (Library of Congress, Washing-
    ton), x, 69; *Freeman's Journal*, 26 May 1778.
17 Coyle, 'Newenham', pp. 25–8; Dixon Webster, 'Benjamin Franklin and an Irish
    "enthusiast" ', *Huntington Library Quarterly* (1940–41), iv, pp. 2067; *Freeman's Jour-
    nal*, 4 June 1778.

However, it became clear when Gardiner's measure was given its first reading on 5 June that stalwarts of the Presbyterian cause such as Newenham, Rowley and James Wilson were not equally forthcoming.[18] There is some uncertainty as to whether their priority was to resist Catholic or to advance Presbyterian relief, but they were identifiably ill-at-ease with the mounting evidence that Dublin Castle was predisposed to favour Catholics over dissenters, for on Tuesday, 9 June, Isaac Corry proposed, and Newenham seconded a motion which sought permission to introduce 'a clause or clauses for the relief of His Majesty's Dissenting Protestant subjects' into Gardiner's bill. The reason Newenham gave for favouring this *modus operandi* over a separate bill, when he requested that the previous order of the House authorising him to prepare a bill for the relief of Protestant dissenters should be discharged, was that the 'shortness of time' remaining in the session prevented him from 'framing so extensive and useful a bill' that would relieve them from both the Test oath and the obligation to pay tithe. This was plausible, but few were convinced and the palpable lack of enthusiasm for a proposal that both altered the thrust and threatened to complicate the passage of Gardiner's original measure obliged Corry to 'withdraw his motion for the present'.[19] Newenham was not prepared to let the idea drop, however; two days later he gave formal notice of his intention of moving on 15 June for the insertion of 'a clause in the bill for the relief of the Roman Catholics to repeal the Sacramental Test in the qualification for offices'.[20]

This was most unwelcome news for the proponents of Catholic relief. They felt strongly that the two questions should be treated separately.[21] However, when the House reassembled on Monday, 15 June, Newenham seized the initiative and the moral high ground by declining to make the traditional statement recommending the motion he offered on the grounds that it would 'be an insult to a Protestant House of Commons and to the representatives of Protestants, were I to request their relief to brother Protestants'. He pronounced simply that 'if the Protestants are not relieved it will be a great hardship upon them'.[22]

This was an extremely effective tactic given the protests of those who supported Catholic relief that they did not seek to undermine the 'Protestant interest' in any way. However, because the incorporation of a provision for the repeal of the Test increased the risk of the relief bill being lost by intensifying opposition, among the Church of Ireland episcopacy in the Lords

18 HMC, *Stopford-Sackville MSS* (2 vols, London, 1904–10), i, p. 250; Burns 'Catholic relief', p. 193; *Freeman's Journal*, 9 June 1778; *Commons, Jn. (Irl.)*, ix, 482, 493; Cavendish's parl. diary, x, 231.
19 *Freeman's Journal*, 11 June 1778.
20 Cavendish's parl. diary, x, 261; *Freeman's Journal*, 13 June 1778.
21 Cavendish's parl. diary, x, 261.
22 Ibid., xi, 1.

and some peers and bishops on the Privy Council, they had little option but
to oppose Newenham's motion. He maintained, in response to the claim by
Sir Henry Cavendish, MP for Lismore, that 'the tacking of this clause ... will
be a clog' that he had no wish to encumber the Catholic relief bill. He
professed that his preferred *modus operandi* was to address the subjects of
Catholic and Presbyterian relief separately. At the same time, he was not
entirely consistent since he admitted that he was opposed to what he described as 'a partial repeal' which relieved only one denomination, and that
he had only decided to adopt this mode of proceeding when he realised that
a bill for Presbyterian relief was 'not liable to be successful'. This did little to
ease the anxieties of committed proponents of Catholic relief like Luke Gardiner
and Barry Barry. Barry most forcefully expressed the conviction that
Newenham's primary motive was 'to obstruct' Catholic relief, but James
Wilson, Thomas Conolly, John Scott (the attorney general), Lucius O'Brien
and others (for different reasons) endorsed his contention that it was both
impolitic and inappropriate to link the two issues. However, a majority of
MPs who favoured the repeal of the Sacramental Test (and a strong majority of
those who spoke did) had no objection to admitting the clause into the bill.
They included the Provost, John Hely-Hutchinson, the Prime Serjeant, Hussey
Burgh, and, significantly, prominent MPs from Ulster, notably James Stewart
(County Tyrone), Armor Lowry Corry (County Tyrone), Alexander
Montgomery, (County Donegal) and Barry Yelverton (Donegal borough). As a
result, Newenham's proposal was ratified without a division.[23]

Pursuant to this decision, Newenham moved on 19 June that the committee
considering the Catholic relief bill should receive a clause to repeal the Sacramental Test. He had to overcome more determined opposition on this occasion
because, in the days following his success in securing the permission of the
house to offer such a clause, the leaders of the Castle interest in the Commons
had concluded that they had erred in not resisting the suggestion on 15 June.
The Provost signalled their change of heart by indicating that he was no longer
prepared to support the inclusion of a clause repealing the Sacramental Test in
a bill whose primary object was Catholic relief. The attorney general was more
forceful. He urged MPs not to accept the clause on the grounds that it was 'the
direct way to annihilate both' Catholic and Presbyterian relief:

> I think it not right to put it as a rider to another bill; if right it ought to
> force itself; if wrong it ought not to crush an harmless brother; ... it has power-ful
> opponents on this side of the water; it had enemies there; an attempt has
> been made in Great Britain; it has often failed; where churchmen think
> the peace of the Church depends upon it, where statesmen think the

23 Cavendish's parl. diary, xi, 1–64; *Freeman's Journal*, 16, 18 June 1778; *Commons
   Jn. (Irl.)*, ix, 493; Burns, 'Catholic relief', p. 193.

> peace of the state depends on it whether as a friend to the Popery part
> or to what the Protestant Dissenters at present, it may ruin itself....

This was exceptionally blunt, given the attorney general's dislike of the Catholic relief bill, but it did not persuade a majority of those present to change their minds. The combined numbers of those 'friends of government [who] were inclined to favour the Presbyterians on this occasion', of the pro-Presbyterian interest and the anti-Catholic borough interests of Lord Shannon and Lord Ely, who believed the clause would serve 'as a clogg upon the whole of the bill', ensured that Newenham's clause was received and read. Indeed, not just this but, at three a.m., his request that the title of the bill should be amended to include the phrase 'and for other purposes' to signal it no longer related solely to Catholics was approved.[24]

The relative ease with which Newenham secured the backing of the House of Commons for his scheme to repeal the Sacramental Test disturbed the rainbow of interests that favoured Catholic relief. They watched with mounting unease, the Lord Lieutenant, the Earl of Buckinghamshire, reported, MPs opposed to the bill vote for the clause in the expectation that it would result in the rejection of the measure by the Commons when it was returned from England minus 'the dissenter clause'. Realising this, Barry Barry invited MPs not to perceive this outcome as an insult to Ireland' in the debate on the report stage on 20 June. This was unusual, but he and other critics of the clause knew there was nothing to be gained by prolonging the debate on the bill in the House of Commons. The opponents of Catholic relief had arrived at the same conclusion, with the result that the Speaker was able to announce shortly afterwards that it had 'been compromised that if the promoters of the Bill would not oppose the dissenters clause, the opponents would agree to the rest'. The formalities of the final stages were concluded without incident on the same day, and Luke Gardiner was directed to convey the bill to the Earl of Buckinghamshire for transmission in 'due form' to London.[25]

III

The incorporation of a clause repealing the Sacramental Test into the heads of a bill whose origins and prime object was Catholic relief was heartening for the number of proponents of Presbyterian relief in the House of Commons,

24 Cavendish's parl.diary, xii, 284-98; *Freeman's Journal*, 23 June; National Archives, [hereafter NA], Irish Correspondence 1697–1782, Ms 2447 ff.208–10; Public Record Office Northern Ireland, [hereafter PRONI] Normanton Papers, T3719/C/12/44; Burns, 'Catholic relief', p 198; HMC, *Stopford-Sackville Mss*, i, p. 251.
25 Cavendish's parl. diary, xiii, 306-34; *Freeman's Journal*, 23 June; NA, Irish Correspondence, MS 2447 ff.208–10; Burns, 'Catholic relief', p 198.

but they were acutely aware that the bill still had formidable obstacles to overcome if it was to become law. They had only managed to progress this far because of the support of a substantial number of MPs who calculated that the inclusion of the Sacramental Test clause would ensure the rejection of Catholic relief. Its opponents did not believe that the Irish or British Privy Councils would come to their rescue and respite the measure, but this did not trouble them much. They were confident that whatever happened they could not lose; because if one of the councils 'expung[ed]' the test clause, the Irish House of Commons would reject it on its return from England, and if both left it unaltered 'the whole bill would upon that account be rejected by the House of Lords'. Buckinghamshire was anxious that this should not happen though he had not put his authority on the line on the matter. He had, he informed a close friend, 'take[n] nothing upon myself' because 'no line of conduct was absolutely prescribed'. Indeed, he 'did not think [him]self competent to form a firm judgement of my own' on the issues raised by the bill, and he relied for guidance on the Primate, Richard Robinson, Lord Chancellor Lifford, and Lord Annaly. It is not clear if they spoke with one voice, but it suited them that London's instructions were to favour Catholic and not dissenter relief because they feared that the already frail Castle interest might be weakened further if the Irish Privy Council was left free to decide the matter.[26]

The meeting of the Irish Privy Council on 25 June to consider the relief bill provided some of the most powerful temporal and spiritual Lords in the kingdom with their first opportunity to express their views on a measure many Protestants believed now posed a dual threat to their ascendancy. The antipathy of Lords Shannon and Ely to Catholic relief had been clearly signalled; the addition of the provision to repeal the Sacramental Test distressed the more reserved Church of Ireland hierarchy, and its members on the Council Board did not hesitate to make their reservations known. They were joined in their opposition by the Attorney-General; but, like those 'Lords of great weight and consequence' who had to accept they did not have the votes to throw out 'the whole of the bill', both he and the bishops had to concede that they too could not achieve their object. This was due in part to the unwillingness of some councillors to provoke a political crisis by acting on their convictions. The Lord Lieutenant observed in his report to London that 'a much greater number would have appeared against the Presbyterian clause, if they had not conceived that it might be more properly rejected in

26 Public Record Office, [hereafter PRO] , SP 63/460 ff.143, 160; NA, Irish Correspondence, 1697–1782, MS 2447 ff.268–70; Bartlett, *Fall and rise*, p. 88; PRONI, Hotham Papers, T3429/1/33; Buckinghamshire to North, Buckinghamshire to Germain, 25, 21 June 1778, National Library Ireland, [hereafter NLI], Heron Papers, MSS 13036/12, 13052/2).

England than on this side'. Evidently, he was not the only one who was relieved that the fate of the bill was now ministerial responsibility.[27]

Despite his unwillingness actively to support the bill, Buckinghamshire was not neutral about its fate. He transmitted it to London 'without waiting for any other to accompany it, in order that it may be the more speedily taken into consideration by his Majesty and his Privy Council', and he sent reports of what had transpired at the Irish Council to Lords Gower and Germain in addition to Lord Weymouth, the secretary of state responsible for Irish affairs.[28]

Buckinghamshire's concern for the bill was prompted in part by the busy round of speculation in Ireland as to whether it would be returned from England, and its fate if it was received with or without the Sacramental Test clause.[29] He was also aware that it had many powerful enemies in England, and his anxiety on this score was heightened by news from the Secretary at War, Charles Jenkinson, that 'a violent attempt [was being] made through *Irish influence* to have it rejected in England'. Jenkinson's report is short on details. But it is hardly coincidental that his claim that among the bill's most active opponents were some 'who did not at first chuse to appear against it and were anxious that it should be stifled with us' concurs with the Lord Lieutenant's report of proceedings at the Irish Council. It also suggests that they numbered more than just Church of Ireland bishops.[30] Their object was to induce cabinet ministers and privy councillors, hostile to relieving dissenters, to oppose the bill on the grounds that it went further than the British parliament was prepared to go. They were obliged to work quickly because upon receipt of the bill, Lord Weymouth promptly transmitted it to the attorney and solicitor generals (Alexander Wedderburn and James Wallace) so they could get on with preparing their report for the Irish bills' committee of the Privy Council.[31]

The efforts of the bill's Irish critics to excite opposition to the measure in London forced Catholic well-wishers to take counter-measures. Edmund Burke, who played an important role in smoothing the way for Catholic relief, was on record as stating that a bill whose main feature was its 'simplicity and plainness' would find greatest favour. He did not anticipate, when he made this remark, that the repeal of the Sacramental Test, towards which he was well-inclined, would become 'mix[ed]' with the question of Catholic relief because the two

27 Buckinghamshire to North, 21 June, NLI, Heron Papers, MS 13036/12; Burns, 'Catholic relief', pp. 198–9; PRO, Granville Papers, 30/29/3/9; PRO, SP 63/460 f.279; HMC, *Stopford-Sackville*, i, 251.
28 Buckinghamshire to Germain, 25 June, NLI, Heron Papers, MS 13052/2; PRO, Granville Papers, 30/29/3/9; PRO, SP 63/460 f.279.
29 H.M.C., *Stopford Sackville Mss*, i, 251; Buckinghamshire to Germain, 6 July 1778, NLI, Heron Papers, MS 13052/2.
30 British Library, Liverpool Papers, Add. MS 38206 f.93.
31 PRO, Privy Council Papers, PC 2/122; Bartlett, *Fall and rise*, p. 89.

'cause[s]' were 'so different', so when he learned that they were 'mix[ed]' he appreciated the seriousness of the threat it posed Catholic relief. It was, he ventured, impolitic for Ireland to run ahead of Britain and the opinion of 'the dissenters in England', and 'impracticable' as well as 'ill intended' to press for 'the repeal of the Test' at this moment. He anticipated that, at the very least, the clause repealing the Sacramental Test could be deleted and, like Barry Barry, he sought to convince Irish opinion to accept that the 'alterations' to the bill were not aimed to 'hurt ... your parliamentary dignity'.[32]

Burke did this despite the fact that when, on 2 July, he was invited by Attorney General Wedderburn to send him his 'thoughts of the Irish Toleration bill and particularly of the dissenters' clause', he recommended that the bill should pass the British Privy Council unaltered. Conceiving that the best way to ensure Catholic relief was 'to recommend the *whole*', Burke made light of 'the objections to that part that related to the dissenters with regard both to the general propriety and to the temporary policy at this juncture'.[33] Indeed, he sought out the Solicitor General and Lord Chancellor Thurlow, to impress the point upon them. He also lobbied Sir Grey Cooper, the influential joint secretary at the Treasury, and the prime minister, Lord North, who did not mask his antipathy to the proposal to repeal the Sacramental Test. North insisted 'that his ideas of toleration were large, but that, large as they were, they did not comprehend a promiscuous establishment, even in matters merely civil; — ... he thought the established religion ought to be the religion of the state'. The fact that Britain's dissenters had not requested the repeal of the test reinforced the prime minister's conviction, but as Burke reported, 'the thing which seemed to affect him most, was the offence that would be taken by the repeal by the leaders among the church clergy here, on one hand, and, on the other, the steps which would be taken for its repeal in England in the next session, in consequence of the repeal in Ireland'. Burke sought to assure him that the Whigs would not agitate the point, but the prime minister was unimpressed. He undertook to consider repealing 'the test *quoad* military and revenue offices', thereby leaving 'church and civil government' unaltered (a concession recommended by his Irish-born adviser William Knox), but he was unwilling to go further even if it meant endangering Catholic relief, and upsetting figures as diverse as Edmund Pery, Robert, Earl Nugent and Hervey, the Earl-Bishop of Derry who, in Pery's words, maintained that Catholic relief would be 'a very great acquisition'. The fate of the measure lay very much in the balance as a result. And the largest quotient of doubt hovered over the clause for the repeal of the test because of ministerial resistance to the proposition and to their wish not to

32 G.H.Guttridge and J.A.Woods (eds), *The correspondence of Edmund Burke* (vols iii and iv, Cambridge, 1961–3), iii, pp. 455–6, 461–2, 464–5, iv, pp. 3–4.
33 Woods, ed., *The correspondence of Burke*, iv, pp. 5–6.

be seen to encourage a 'confederacy, real or apparent' of Catholics and dissenters.[34] There was, as we know, no 'confederacy' or any prospect of such at this time. But the fact that it was suggested highlights the level of unease in British political circles with the bill. News reports, a week before the bill was scheduled for consideration by the Privy Council on 23 July, that the Attorney General's report was positive might have been expected to have eased the anxieties of its supporters, but this was negated by the decision of Lord Gower, who was 'a friend' to go 'into the country'.[35] Moreover, the joint report of the law officers presented to the Irish bills' committee was not uncritical. They were unhappy, for example, with the provision that Catholics should be allowed to make 999 year leases but not to purchase land on fee simple. More consequentially, they described the clause repealing the Sacramental Test as of little value because 'there are few or none who can gain any personal advantage' by its repeal. But because they had been informed by Edmund Burke, and others, that any interference with the clause would 'endanger the success of a bill so strongly recommended by every consideration of wisdom and humanity', they made no recommendation as to its fate.[36]

Unfortunately, no record of the discussion of the bill at the Privy Council survives. The only clue we have as to what transpired is provided by William Knox who reported that the decision to return the bill without 'the tacked clause for repeal of the test' was 'obtained with much difficulty'.[37] This is profoundly disappointing, because we cannot establish if the source of the 'difficulty' a difference between those who favoured retaining the dissenter clause and those who urged its deletion.

What is indisputable is that the bill was anxiously awaited in Ireland. It was the subject of such persistent speculation that when Richard Heron confirmed the rumours that the bill would be returned minus the Sacramental Test clause in the House of Commons on Monday, 27 July, calls were immediately raised for the 'true' friends of the country 'to unite to defeat the arbitrary intentions of our rulers by throwing out this ominous bill' and attempts made to excite ancient Protestant fears of Catholic rebellion and massacre.[38] The *ad hoc* coalition of anti-Catholic and pro-dissenter interests

34 Ibid., pp. 6–10; Knox to Heron, 6, 16 July 1778 Royal Irish Academy, [hereafter RIA], Knox Letters, MS G. 5 .1); J.P. Day, 'The Catholic question in the Irish parliament 1760–82'MA thesis, National University of Ireland, University College Dublin, 1973, p 137.
35 Knox to Heron, 16 July 1778, RIA, Knox Letters, MS G. 5. 1.
36 Bartlett, *Fall and rise*, p 89; Day, 'Irish Catholics', pp. 136–7.
37 Knox to Heron, 23 July, RIA, Knox Letters, MS G. 5. 1; PRO, Privy Council Papers, PC 2/122 ff.316–7, 354–5; PRO, SP 63/460 ff.354–6.
38 *Freeman's Journal*, 2, 11, 16, 23, 30 July; NA, Irish Correspondence, 1697–1798, MS 2447 f.277; Cavendish's parl. diary, xiii, p. 21.

that had come together to support the 'dissenters clause' was reformed. They were determined to resist the ratification of the bill and they signalled their intention on 27 July when they made it clear that they would move for a committee of comparison—a procedure usually reserved for money bills—to established formally where the bill differed from the heads they had ratified. Speaker Pery was confident, nonetheless, that the administration would prevail if the Lord Lieutenant and Chief Secretary rallied the Castle interest and ignored the rumours that the rejection of the bill would force the unpopular Buckinghamshire's resignation.[39]

Pery was proved correct. When the House of Commons assembled on Monday, 3 August, a committee of comparison was established. It reported on the following day that 'several alterations' had been made to the 'heads' they had transmitted. This was the opportunity the proponents of Presbyterian relief awaited, and guided by Sir Richard Johnston, MP for Kilbeggan, and George Ogle, the anti-Catholic diehard from County Wexford, they moved to have the test clause reinserted. This was contrary to the rule and practice of the House, and though a number of impressive statements were made in favour of relieving dissenters the Speaker ruled the motion out of order.[40]

This signalled the end of the 1778 campaign to repeal the Sacramental Test, though it did not conclude debate on the issue. Following the rejection of the attempt to have the 'dissenters clause' reinserted in the bill, George Ogle sought to kill the measure by proposing that its committal be scheduled for 1 November. This prompted a long and emotional debate in which concern for the future security of the Protestant interest and support for the repeal of the Sacramental Test was widely voiced, and in which Sir Edward Newenham and Thomas Conolly had a sharp exchange over the former's appeal to dissenters in Ulster for instructions on how they preferred to be relieved. There was, as both men were fully aware, now no prospect of doing anything in the current session, and the rejection of motions by George Ogle on 3 August and by Sir Richard Johnston two days later calling for the repeal of the Sacramental Test merely emphasized the fact. Hopes were high for 1779–80, though a suggestion that it would encounter less resistance if it was annexed to a money bill indicated that some believed that desperate remedies were called for.[41] Sir Edward Newenham and his allies had failed to secure the repeal of the Sacramental Test in 1778; they were determined they would be more successful next time.

39 Cavendish's parl.diary, xiii, pp. 21-5; Burns, 'Catholic relief', p 199; Bartlett, *Fall and rise*, pp. 89–90; PRONI, Normanton Papers, T 3719/C/12/11.
40 Cavendish's parl. diary, xiii, 44, 138–59; *Commons Jn. (Irl.)*, ix, 515; Burns, 'Catholic relief', pp. 199–200.
41 Cavendish's parl.diary, xiii, pp. 159-348; *Commons Jn. (Irl.)*, ix, 515; Burns, 'Catholic relief', pp. 199–203; Bartlett, *Fall and rise*, p. 90

IV

Despite the stir the attempt to repeal the Sacramental Test occasioned in 1778, the issue was not accorded a prominent public airing in the interval between the conclusion of the 1777–78 session and the reconvening of parliament in October 1779. Yet a complex of factors combined to ensure that legislation to rescind the test became law during this session. The fact that the position of Catholics had been eased was crucial. There was no *a priori* reason why this should facilitate Presbyterian expectations, but only the most zealous devotees of the Church of Ireland remained convinced that it was appropriate to retain the existing disabilities against Presbyterians when those against Catholics were being ameliorated. Indeed, prominent people in the political mainstream in Britain as well as Ireland shared the opinion of Edmund Burke (as conveyed to Luke Gardiner) that 'the scheme of toleration can never be compleated up to the standard of your equitable and liberal ideas' until the dissenters grievances were also addressed.[42] There was little appetite in ministerial circles to yield them extensive concessions for, among other reasons, 'their strong predilection to the American rebels', but Britain's declining military fortunes in the colonies combined with the greater assertiveness of Irish Presbyterian opinion in 1779 to ensure that their grievances were afforded a more sympathetic response.[43]

The most visible indicator of the difficulties the Presbyterians could occasion was provided by their enthusiastic embrace of Volunteering. The transformation of the Volunteers from a modest civilian militia into a formidable paramilitary force in 1778–9 frightened many in positions of influence and authority in Ireland, and they did not shirk from conveying their anxiety to London. Philip Skelton, for example, informed William Knox in October 1779 that

> the dissenters, most warmly, have taken up arms, which they now threaten to use against England. They will not so much as drink success to his Majesty's fleet against the fleets of France and Spain, on which two powers they depend for aid against England; and hardly at all disguise their intention to play off the American hand of cards, up from duces to aces. It is in vain to remonstrate that independency here must be impossible without the total reduction of England; that this cannot be effected without the aid of French and Spanish forces, or that France and Spain, in case England is once ruined, must be paid by a subjection of Ireland to those arbitrary powers; without, in short,

---

42 Woods, (ed.), *Burke Corres.*, iv, pp. 17–18.
43 HMC, *Stopford-Sackville Mss*, i, pp. 260–1; Thomas Bartlett, 'The origins and progress of the Catholic question' in Thomas Power and Kevin Whelan, (eds), *Endurance and emergence* (Dublin, 1990), p. 10; McBride, 'Presbyterianism', pp. 82–3.

the fate of Corsica ... They will listen to no sober counsels. They give
out that they have 30,000 men well armed and disciplined, and begin
already to insult the army and our chief governor.

In Skelton's estimation, 'concessions' were essential if 'the trumpet of rebellion ... loudly blown by the dissenting ministers of Ulster' was to be 'qui-
eted'.[44] Lord Buckinghamshire concurred. He informed his ministerial colleagues in London that the administration could evade sponsoring legislation
to relieve the dissenters because Edward Newenham had let it be known that
he would propose 'Heads of a bill ... of the same nature as the clause rejected'
in 1778 once parliament resumed, but he believed it was to their advantage to
support such an initiative, and a meeting of Belfast Presbyterians in October
at which a petition condemning government partiality and asserting their
entitlement to 'all the rights of free-born subjects' confirmed him in this
opinion.[45] Indeed, prior to the opening of the session, he directed Sir Richard
Heron to seek 'instructions' on the matter from Lord Weymouth. But no
reply had been received by the time MPs convened in October.[46]

In the absence of guidance from London, the initiative on the issue of repealing the Sacramental Test remained, where it had rested in 1778, with the
pro-Presbyterian interest in the House of Commons. True to his word, Sir
Edward Newenham 'moved for leave to bring in the heads of a bill for the relief
of his Majesty's most faithful and loyal dissenting subjects' on the opening day
of the session. Leave was given without hesitation and a committee comprising
himself, Thomas Conolly, Barry Yelverton, Sir Richard Johnston and Isaac Corry
was ordered to prepare a bill.[47] It was the first stage of what was to prove a most
uneventful Commons' passage. Newenham presented the heads of a bill providing for the repeal of the offending clause from the 1704 act to prevent the
further growth of Popery to the House on 15 November. Since 'great numbers
of those members who had opposed it last session' were 'pledged' to support it
on this occasion, it met with no obstruction. The measure sailed through its
various reading and committee stages without an amendment being tabled, and
it was ready for presentation to the Lord Lieutenant a mere twelve days later.[48]

It was at this point that the fortunes of the measure became decidedly more
troubled. Because he had still not received any instructions from London (for
which he made a further request on 2 December) as to how he should respond
to the bill, Buckinghamshire was unsure what to do. His wish was to facilitate

44 HMC, *Knox Papers*, pp. 447–8.
45 McBride, 'Presbyterians', p. 83.
46 PRO, SP, 63/467 ff.188–90, 295–6.
47 *Freeman's Journal*, 14 Oct.; *Commons Jn. (Irl.)*, x, pp. 11, 13; PRO, SP 63/467 ff.190–1.
48 PRO, SP, 63/467 ff.190–1; *Freeman's Journal*, 16 November 1779; *Commons Jn. (Irl.)*, x,
    pp. 24, 29–30, 35, 37.

its progress, because the overwhelming support of MPs for the measure suggested that it would rebound on the Castle in the Commons if he did otherwise, but government support was vital to enable him to overcome episcopal resistance at the Irish Privy Council. He bought himself a few days by not making himself available to receive the bill until 2 December, but the expectation that the Council would complete its consideration of the bill within a week gave him little room to manoeuvre.[49] Obliged to refer the bill to the Council, he immediately ran into opposition from a well-organized Church of Ireland lobby which was emboldened by the advice of the well-connected English MP Welbore Ellis, and the former chief secretary, Sir George Macartney to oppose any 'meddling with any of the laws concerning religion'. They argued their case with such passion that the Council split, Buckinghamshire reported on 21 December, between those—the Lord Chancellor, Attorney General and John Foster - who favoured transmitting the bill and those—'the Church'—who were 'very adverse'.[50]

The recalcitrance of the Council troubled Buckinghamshire, who was relying on the bill 'to quiet the spirit of the most dangerous body in this kingdom'—Ulster Presbyterians. He did not possess the authority to carry the matter over the objections of its clerical critics so he and Speaker Edmund Pery sought to impress upon ministers that a 'constitutional' crisis would ensue if it was 'stifled' in the Irish Council. Lord North was 'distress[ed]' that a measure he disliked had been allowed to proceed so far, but perceiving no alternative but to acquiesce in what was being asked of him, he reluctantly conceded in early January that the government would use its influence to ensure that the test bill negotiated the British Privy Council. This was precisely what Buckinghamshire and Pery wanted to hear, and when they learned in early January that the government had decided 'to let our test bill pass' they determined to press the matter to a successful resolution without delay. The act to relieve dissenters was, as Pery noted, the price that had to be paid to 'deprive men of ill intentions of an instrument with which they may do much mischief'.[51] Not surprisingly, when the Irish Privy Council considered the 'dissenter bill' on 21 January, it was approved and ordered to be transmitted to London.[52]

This was a setback for the mainly clerical opponents of the repeal of the Sacramental Test. But they were encouraged by George Macartney's reports to Charles Agar, the newly appointed bishop of Cashel, of Lord North's dissatisfaction with the pressure he was put under to conclude that if they could provide the prime minister with 'good grounds for refusing to return the bill to

49 PRO, SP 63/467 ff.190–1; *Commons Jn. (Irl.)*, x, p. 47; *Freeman's Journal*, 2 December 1779.
50 PRO, SP 63/467 ff.295–6; PRONI, Normanton Papers, T 3719/C/13/46, 14/4.
51 H.M.C., *Emly*, p. 207; PRO, SP, 63/467 ff.295–6, 468 f.15; HMC, *Lothian*, p. 360; Thomas Bartlett (ed.), *Macartney in Ireland 1767–72* (Belfast, 1978) p. 326.
52 PRO, SP 63/468 f.96.

you' he would ensure its rejection at the British Council board. Macartney advised that this could be best achieved by the time honoured device of petitioning. Spurred on by this, Agar sought immediately to galvanize opposition in clerical and political quarters in Britain as well as Ireland.[53] As in 1778, the opponents of the bill had little time to rally support, so Agar's first move was to request Macartney to encourage the prime minister to delay consideration of the bill by the British Privy Council. He also used his connection with Welbore Ellis to communicate the depth of clerical opposition to Lord North, while he explored the practicalities of organizing a petition from the clergy and a protest from the bishops of the Church of Ireland 'as the guardians of the rights of the Church and of the established religion'. This two-pronged strategy proved more 'difficult' to implement than he had anticipated. And following consultations with Primate Robinson, who was eager to do whatever he could to resist the bill and aid Lord North, he confined his efforts to lobbying the Church of Ireland bishops to put their name to 'a joint letter to the Archbishop of Canterbury' in which they requested him

> to use his endeavours in the Privy Council of England to suppress the bill if that be possible, but should he fail in that to have it altered by the addition to the end of the bill which substitutes a *declaration* to be made by every person in lieu of the Sacramental Test.

This 'declaration' sought to commit all officeholders to agree to profess 'that I do not believe the public worship of the Church of Ireland as by law established to be sinful or idolatrous' and it won the backing, as well as Agar and Robinson, of Robert Fowler, archbishop of Dublin, Jemmet Browne, archbishop of Tuam and ten bishops.[54]

Given the enthusiasm in episcopal circles for this formula and their understanding that Lord North was looking for reasons to resist the repeal of the test, Agar and Robinson might reasonably have anticipated that it would have influenced the Privy Council's deliberations, but it was not to be. The government had already made up its mind to sanction the measure, and as soon as he received the bill, the secretary of state, Lord Hillsborough, ensured it was considered 'with all possible dispatch'. More significantly, the Crown's law officers found nothing objectionable in the measure when they reported on 22 February. Seven days later the Irish bills' committee endorsed their opinion and

---

53 Bartlett, (ed.), *Macartney*, p. 326; PRONI, Chilham Papers, T 2519/4/8.
54 Bartlett (ed.), *Macartney in Ireland*, pp. 326–30; PRONI, Normanton Papers, T3719/ C/14/5; HMC, *Stopford-Sackville Mss.*, i, 267–8. The bishops were Kildare, Clogher, Cork and Ross, Leighlin and Ferns, Kilmore, Dromore, Meath, Limerick, Elphin and Clonfert. Hervey, Bishop of Derry was the one bishop who supported the relief of dissenters.

when the full council did likewise on 1 March, it was passed under the great seal and a commission ordered to authorise the Lord Lieutenant of Ireland to give it royal approval if it was passed unaltered by both house of the Irish parliament.[55]

Lord Hillsborough observed in the dispatch accompanying the return of 'the dissenters relief bill' that he and other ministers anticipated that the 'great satisfaction' it would give 'to a very numerous and respectable body of His Majesty's subjects' would aid the Lord Lieutenant to resist any attempt that might be made to agitate constitutional points and pave the way for the restoration of 'general harmony'. The bill was certainly afforded a positive welcome on its return, and it completed all its stages uneventfully in the Commons and Lords between 11 April and 2 May, when it received the royal assent.[56]

V

The government's hope that the repeal of the Sacramental Test would cause the Presbyterians to abandon political agitation proved unfounded. They went on to play so central part in the campaigns for legislative independence and renunciation that Belfast was described by one hostile observer in August 1782 as 'a perfect Boston'.[57] From the point of view of a majority of Presbyterians this was entirely legitimate because the repeal of the Sacramental Test was less consequential than free trade, legislative independence, renunciation and parliamentary reform. Their object in the late 1770s and early 1780s was less relief from sectarian discrimination than the political empowerment of the kingdom of Ireland in its relationship with Britain and their full inclusion in the political process. The former was largely secured between 1778 and 1783; the latter was denied because of the resistance of the Church of Ireland elite to any dilution of its command of the power structures.[58] However, legislation introduced by Ulster MPs did secure the further dilution of the disabilities under which they conducted their lives. In 1782, the prohibition on Presbyterian ministers marrying members of their own communion was lifted despite the determined opposition of the Church of Ireland hierarchy, while partial relief was allowed the seceders for 'their refusal to conform to the common mode of swearing by kissing the Bible'. Two years later, the *regium donum* was increased though not by enough to provide each minister with the targeted £40.[59] For moderates, like William

55 PRO, SP 63/468 f.114; PRO, PC 1/12/7, 2/124 ff.585–6, 2/125 ff.1–2.
56 PRO, SP 63/468 ff.320–2; *Commons Jn. (Irl.)*, x, 85, 89, 91, 95, 118, 119.
57 Lord Herbert (ed.), *Pembroke papers 1734–91* (2 vols, London, 1939–50), ii, 203.
58 McDowell, *Ireland in the age of imperialism*, pp. 310–13; Kelly, 'Parliamentary reform', pp. 78–86.
59 Reid, *History of the Presbyterian Church*, iii, 347–8; HMC, *Charlemont*, ii, 1–4, 7–8, 16–7, 25–6; R.I.A., Charlemont Papers, Ms 12 R 14/12.

Campbell, the minister at Armagh who disliked public agitation, it was sufficient reason for Presbyterians to continue to work the political system. The problem was that the anti-Presbyterian prejudice that had sustained the Sacramental
Test for so long remained alive within the Church of Ireland elite. Campbell
failed to advance plans for a Presbyterian college, for example. More dramati-
cally, he was personally to experience it when he was provoked into entering the
'paper war' of the mid-1780s by the accusation by Bishop Richard Woodward of
Cloyne that Presbyterian allegiance to the state was less than complete.[60] He and
others vigorously reprobated this claim. But the fact that it was made, and that
the repeal of the Sacramental Test a few years earlier was due, in large part, to
the conviction of Sir Edward Newenham that Catholics should not be advan-
taged compared to Presbyterians and to the security concerns of the British government emphasises the continuing depth of the reservoir of antipathy to dissent that existed within episcopalian Protestantism in eighteenth-century Ireland.

60 James Kelly, 'Relations between the Protestant Church of Ireland and the Presbyterian
Church in late eighteenth-century Ireland', *Eire–Ireland*, 23(1988), pp. 38–56.

I wish to thank Dr David Hayton for his comments and advice.

John Wesley's Political Sensibilities in Ireland, 1747–89

ROBIN RODDIE

On Thursday 29 April 1762 John Wesley with two of his itinerant preachers arrived in Monaghan and booked into the *King's Arms*. No sooner had they arrived than it was reported to the Provost that there were 'three strange sort of men' come to town. The affair might have turned serious,[1] wrote Wesley, had he not fortuitously had in his possession two letters, one from the bishop of Derry, and the other from the earl of Moira. The reason, he discovered, for suspicion at their unexpected arrival was the general alarm caused by the Whiteboy commotions of Munster. There the matter might have rested but it was not in the nature of Wesley to ignore issues of such general interest particularly when they came so close to affecting his itinerary. Six weeks later when he got to Cork he was able to get 'an exact account of the Whiteboys'. In his journal he gave what he called a 'plain, naked account of what had been so variously represented'.[2] It is a brief, dispassionate summary of the origins, methods and apparent suppression of the Whiteboy activity. A fortnight later he arrived in Waterford just in time to follow-up with a report on the execution of four of the Whiteboys.[3]

This unexpected and very personal encounter by Wesley with the emergence of eighteenth-century agrarian protest in Ireland will serve as an introduction to the wider theme of Wesley's political sensitivity in Ireland. On the evidence of this brief extract from Wesley's own journal, at this stage in the middle of his ninth tour and with another eleven to follow it appears on the surface that he had established some acceptance among both Church of Ireland leaders and the gentry, most of whom were part of the established church. However, he had developed only a limited interest in Irish political activities. Wesley was reluctant to engage personally in high politics, therefore this chapter is concerned primarily with the political attitude he had toward late eighteenth-century Irish society.

---

1 W.R. Ward and R.P. Heitzenrater (eds) *Journal and diaries of John Wesley* [hereafter *JDJW*] (7 vols, Nashville, 1988–97) iv, p. 363.
2 *JDJW*, iv. p. 368.
3 Ibid., iv, p. 373.

I

John Wesley was not the first Methodist, nor even the first Methodist leader, to visit Ireland, but he was the most important. At the time of his arrival in 1747 he was aged forty-four and his political and religious attitudes were largely set. He was by birth, experience and education politically conservative. Born of parents who themselves were loyal to Church and crown, growing up at a time of relative political stability and educated at Oxford, Wesley never had reason to question his understanding of the scriptural injunction to obey the powers-that-be. It made sense of his own experience. Likewise, he was a loyal Churchman. His own long spiritual pilgrimage led him through Catholic mysticism, Continental pietism and a Lutheran version of Calvinism, but he arrived back where he started with a new understanding and appreciation of the Church of England.[4] He brought with him also a pattern of Methodism which had taken shape in the context of England where the established church was also the majority church. Wesleys Irish experience would test that model and challenge its flexibility.

His initial impressions of Ireland were favourable. Writing to his friend and confidant, the London banker Ebenezer Blackwell, he noted that 'all I converse with are only English transplanted into another soil; and they are much mended by the removal, having left all their roughness and surliness behind them'.[5] That opinion he had reason to modify. More significant in the light of subsequent experience he complained.

> At least ninety-nine in a hundred of the native Irish remain in the religion of their forefathers. The Protestants whether in Dublin or elsewhere, are almost all transplanted lately from England. Nor is it any wonder that those who are born Papists generally live and die such, when the Protestants can find no better ways to convert them than the Penal Laws and Acts of Parliament.[6]

II

During Wesley's first visit to Ireland he remained only in Dublin. When he returned the following year he extended his tour into the midlands. On his third visit he nearly got as far as Cork, but for safety reasons due to anti-Methodist riots, was advised to by-pass it. During his subsequent journeys his itinerary

4   For a treatment of Wesley's spiritual development see R.P. Heitzenrater, *Wesley and the people called Methodists* (Nashville, 1995)
5   F. Baker, (ed.), *Letters of John Wesley* [hereafter *LJW*] (2 vols, Oxford, 1980–82), ii, p. 256.
6   *JDJW*, iii, p. 189.

grew more varied and extensive. However, those first visits are important in that they set a pattern and established contacts which gave Wesley's Irish work a dimension which has received some recent attention. His early excursions outside Dublin appear to be determined by the presence of a number of well-connected families whose homes were available and whose evangelical sympathies were already established before he arrived. Those homes continued to remain important so that despite changing demands he almost always included them in his later tours. Through these families he had access to wealthy and influential people who frequently came to his meetings in large numbers. So much so that the editors of the new and definitive edition of *The Works of John Wesley* (still in progress) comment that 'Wesley's self-consciously asserted English mission to the poor was in Ireland refracted through the Protestant gentry class'.[7] They further comment that 'in Ireland his mission worked downward from the gentry class and outward from the garrison in a way that would have been unthinkable in England'.[8]

Others have repeated this verdict,[9] and have also claimed that Wesley 'adopted a strategy of permeating the gentry and garrison in Ireland'.[10] It is, however an assertion that requires a great deal of caution. Concerning the role of the military there is no doubt. Wesley's journals and correspondence provide ample evidence of the importance of soldiers in the early spread of the Methodists in Ireland. The mobility of the lives of the soldiers and in many cases their coming from similar social backgrounds as those of the early itinerant preachers meant that they were in the vanguard of those disseminating Wesley's message. Wesley certainly acknowledged their importance. During a preaching visit to Kilkenny in 1756 he went so far as to write, 'Still in Ireland, the first call is to the soldiery'.[11] More problematic is the suggestion that when he crossed the channel Wesley, either by design or necessity, changed the strategy, direction and focus of his mission. The sheer number of references to gentry and people of quality that he came into contact with is impressive. However, alongside these contacts, Wesley's assessment of the value of these people and the class they represented was frequently expressed in derogatory and extraordinarily harsh language. A closer analysis of Wesley's relationship with the gentry class reveals an uneasy alliance between two distinct strands of evangelicals, especially in his

7   Ibid., i, p. 76.
8   Ibid., i, p. 56.
9   D. Hempton and M. Hill, *Evangelical Protestantism in Ulster society 1740–1890* (London, 1992), p. 2. Cf. D. Hempton, *Methodism and politics in British society 1750–1850*, London 1984, p. 35, 'in the early days, at least, the Methodist message appealed most to a motley crew of Irish Catholic poor, English soldiers and Palatine refugees'.
10 D.W. Bebbington, Review of D. Hempton and M. Hill, *Evangelical Protestantism in Ulster society 1740–1890*, in *Proceedings of the Wesley historical society* (1995), l, p. 58.
11 *JDJW*, iv, p. 53.

early ministry in Ireland. Initially these strands coexisted, but in the 1770s the distinction between Wesley's Arminian theology and the more widely held Calvinistic emphasis sharpened to breaking point. The co-operation that existed earlier, due to coinciding interests, dissipated later. Certainly, Wesley accepted their hospitality and used their homes as important staging posts; providing accommodation for his itinerant preachers, and venues for his conferences. However, although the gentry supported and listened to Wesley they did so on their terms and not his. They were interested in Wesley, the evangelical preacher, but not in Wesley the authoritative leader of a new religious movement. They were not so interested in Wesley's demand for personal self-discipline and a tightly organised grouping of religious societies. They were glad to receive him in their homes and came to listen, as long as it was during a convenient time and there was a conducive atmosphere, but there is no evidence that they joined the Methodist societies in any great numbers either as leaders or ordinary members.

Wesley's ambivalence is palpable. He had more invitations than he could manage or was willing to accept. He was prepared to make some accommodation which allowed for the sensitivities and lifestyles of the gentry, but he always gave the feeling that this was done against his better judgement. His tone was at best one of uneasiness and at worst one of despair. 'At Newmarket', he writes, 'at the request of some of the neighbouring gentry, I deferred preaching till ten o'clock. Many of them were then present and seemed not a little astonished. Perhaps they may remember it—a week'.[12] It was not just their behaviour that provoked such unflattering comments, but more his unease and embarrassment in the presence of people with whom he had little in common. On another occasion, after accepting an invitation to one genteel household he wrote in his journal, 'I was as out of my element, there being no room to talk upon the only subject which deserves the attention of a rational creature'.[13] Surely the conversation there must have been of a more worldly nature than Wesley thought proper.

On the whole it seems that the comparatively large number of references to the gentry during Wesley's Irish tours says more about the nature and composition of Anglican Protestant society in Ireland than any change in attitude or strategy. Their presence, numbers and undoubted interest is deceptive and has to be seen in the context of a more important and more general evangelical awakening, wider than Wesleyan Methodism. As theological controversy sharpened the difference between Calvinist and Arminian strands of the evangelical movement the gentry remained largely outside the Wesleyan religious societies. The most active members and leaders among the late eighteenth-century Methodists were not the gentry. The people whose lives were held up for the edifica-

12 Ibid., iv, p. 60.
13 Ibid., vi, p. 358.

tion of the members of Methodist societies were people like Thomas Jones. He was from Cork and had a natural temper which 'was rough and so was his speech', but nonetheless was, according to Wesley 'a man whom God raised from nothing ... to a plentiful fortune.'[14] Another example is Jane Newland who was from the Liberties in Dublin. She was probably a weaver who as a teenager asked Wesley to put her name down to join as a member. Later, she became a spiritual leader and spent much of her strength in visiting the sick and distressed in hospitals and their homes.[15]

Despite theological controversies, Wesley remained on good if somewhat uneasy terms with Calvinist evangelicals. On his last visit to Dublin he was invited to preach by the Revd Edward Smyth who himself had for a time travelled as a Methodist preacher. Wesley's unease with the worldliness of the gentry was expressed in his journal.

> I accepted of the pressing invitation of Mr Smyth, and preached at Bethesda both morning and evening ... At both times we had a brilliant congregation, among whom were Honourable and Right Honourable persons ... What a mercy it is, what a marvellous condescension in God, to provide such places as Bethesda, and Lady Huntingdon's chapels, for these delicate hearers, who could not bear sound doctrine if it were not set off with these pretty trifles![16]

His lack of desire, or inability, to cultivate contacts with people of political influence in Ireland was in keeping with his professed attitude to politics. But the consequence was political impotence. On at least two occasions when his people in Ireland needed to make legal representations in regard to civil liberties he had to seek help from the Calvinistic Methodists—evangelist George Whitefield and the evangelical patroness, Selina, countess of Huntingdon who had important political connections which she was able to cultivate due to her birth and marriage.

III

Wesley asserted more than once that he was himself no politician,[17] nor was it the place of Christian ministers to preach politics.[18] He believed that preachers

14 Ibid., iv, p. 371.
15 *A short account of the life and death of Jane Newland, of Dublin, who departed this life, October 22, 1789* (London, 1790).
16 N. Curnock (ed.), *Journal of John Wesley* [hereafter *JJW*] (London, 1906–16), vii, p. 485.
17 J. Wesley, *Free thoughts on the present state of public affairs* (London, 1768) in *Works of John Wesley* [hereafter *Works*] (14 vols, London, 1872), xi, p. 14.
18 J. Wesley, *How far is it the duty of a Christian minister to preach politics?* in *Works*, xi, pp. 154–5.

were not competent to do so. However, he did make one exception, he thought that it was the duty of Christian ministers to resist those who set out to weaken the king. He thought it unscriptural to 'speak evil of the ruler of the people'. Notwithstanding his own 'no politics rule' he did allow himself to become involved in political controversy. Two incidents had repercussions, not only for his own reputation, but succeeding generations of Methodists. Religious liberty as it involved measures to relieve Roman Catholics, and the other dealt with political liberty as it affected the people of the North American British colonies.[19] The latter issue is outside the scope of this chapter, and the issue of Wesley's relationship with Roman Catholics will be discussed below. But if Wesley understood politics in general to be outside his province, what did he understand as being his legitimate area of political concern? The answer was tentatively worked out while he was a student at Oxford in the 1730s during the period he later described as 'the first rise of Methodism'. One of those who most influenced him was William Morgan, an Irishman, who has claims to be considered as the first Methodist. Morgan and other members of the Holy Club forged a rigorous spiritual programme. In addition to devotional exercises the programme involved a wide range of charitable activities; helping the poor and aged; schooling for orphan children; and visiting prisons. The programme shaped the work of Wesley's later years and gave a framework to the methodical rules of the religious societies that he formed. These interests were transferred to Ireland as well.

Early on Wesley held strong views on the importance of education though his own experiments did not have happy results. In England he established schools at London (1739), Newcastle (1742) and Kingswood (1748), but they were, even by the standards of the day, harsh and narrow in discipline and reflected a lack of understanding of children or their needs. Of greater importance was the impetus he gave to popular education, the dissemination of inexpensive religious literature, and the promotion of Sunday schools. He applauded and encouraged others in these tasks. In Dublin he saluted the Church of Ireland archbishop of Dublin, Charles Cobbe, for his effort to establish a society for the distribution of books for the poor, saying 'Thanks be to God for this!'[20] He and his brother, Charles, knew better than most of the technical difficulties of printing and distributing literature. They both kept the printers of London, Bristol and Dublin busy and John's circuit riders became both book agents and mobile librarians.

---

19 Joseph Benson, who became one of Wesley's foremost preachers, notes in a letter to Walter Churchey in Hay, Brecknockshire, in 21 May 1776, Wesley's increasing involvement in politics as evidenced in his *Calm Address to the American Colonies* and fears that he is being distracted from more important work. (The Papers of Joseph Benson, John Rylands Library, Manchester, PLP/7/7/5).

20 *JDJW*, iv, p. 141.

In Ireland legal obstacles, designed to ensure that education was in the hands of those who adhered to the Established Church, made it difficult to establish independent schools. Wesley's first attempt was at his Whitefriar Street Chapel, Dublin. When the premises were built in 1750–2, part of the ground was set apart for a free school. Initially classes were held in the lobby of the chapel but a separate Orphan's school was built later. It was attended by some forty boys, who were taught free of charge. Wesley's wider concern for the welfare of children is seen in his reaction to the conditions he found at several of the Charter Schools, the first of which he encountered during a visit to Castlebar in May 1773. The scheme for the schools, established in 1733, was intended as a means of improving the lot of orphaned children. Despite parliamentary grants many of the schools were mismanaged and the scheme, generally, was not successful. All this was too evident at Castlebar. 'The whole', said Wesley, 'was a picture of slothfulness, nastiness, and desolation!'. He described about forty boys and girls walking unaccompanied from church. They were very dirty with stockings about their heels, and many of the girls had holes in their clothes the size of 'crown-pieces'. On his return to Dublin he reported the matter to the trustees of the Charter Schools.[21] He had a similar experience nine years later and also reported it to the trustees. A report following a formal inspection of the schools in 1788 upheld his observations.[22]

Wesley's chief legacy was the impetus set for the founding of schools a generation later. Adam Clarke, native of Antrim, protégé of Wesley, and best Methodist scholar of his time, founded a number of schools and persuaded the British and Foreign Bible Society to publish Bibles in the Irish language. Clarke's work set a pattern for a flowering of Irish Methodist National and Mission schools. In 1861 the census returns showed that the lowest illiteracy rates in Ireland were among the Methodists.

The second thread of sensibility running through Wesley's 'social gospel' was a concern for the relationship between the poor and wealthy. Indeed, he always had a strong bias in favour of the poor that was evident on all levels of his work. In 1773 he wrote, Thoughts on the Present Scarcity of Provisions, where he set out ideas on economic problems. Henry Rack has called this work Wesley's exercise in 'political economy'.[23] Most noteworthy was that Wesley attributed many of the economic ills of the time to the greed and waste of the rich rather than to the more usual culprits of sloth and improvidence of the poor which many evangelicals were prone to do. He so rarely had anything good to say about the wealthy that the few exceptions are all the more noteworthy when they do occur. During one of his visits to Cork he commended the mayor for

21 Ibid., v, p. 368.
22 R.B. Macdowell, *Ireland in the age of imperialism* (Oxford, 1979), p. 158.
23 H.D. Rack, *Reasonable enthusiast, John Wesley and the rise of Methodism* (London, 1989), p. 363.

diverting an annual entertainment budget of £200 toward the relief of the poor freemen and their wives.[24] Similarly in Bandon he commended James Bernard:

> the richest person in these parts, he keeps no race-horses, but loves his wife and home, and spends his time and fortune in improving his estate and employing the poor.[25]

More usual was his recoil at conspicuous wealth and extravagant lifestyles. After visiting the kitchens and dining halls of the Parliament in Dublin he wrote:

> Alas, poor Ireland! Who shall teach thy very senators wisdom? War is ceased, now we are suffering the ills of long continued peace; luxury, more cruel than war, has come upon us.[26]

His sympathies are again demonstrated by his juxtaposition of a description of a genteel congregation at Ennis with a sarcastic reference to 'merciful landlords' whose Palatine tenants despite 'their diligence and frugality' had been forced to immigrate.[27] As it happened it would be from these immigrants that American Methodism would most benefit from Wesley's Irish endeavours.

Wesley always had a strict sense of justice and it was forcefully expressed during his 1773 visit to Belfast, just after the 'Hearts of Steel' disturbances. The immediate cause of the insurrection was the eviction of tenants and imprisonment of one of their number for a refusal to pay what they regarded as unfair 'fines' on the estates of Lord Donegall. Despite his horror of rebellion and fear of instability he demonstrated an understanding of the anger of the protesters who had marched on the city.

> It is no wonder that, as their lives were now bitter to them, they should fly out as they did. It is rather a wonder that they did not go much farther. And if they had, who would have been most in fault? Those who were without home, without money, without food for themselves and families? Or those who drove them to this extremity?[28]

Charitable work with the sick, destitute and imprisoned was the third arm of a life-style which had its roots in Wesley's Oxford days. Ministering to those who were dying, whether from sickness or condemnation, was important so that the message of Divine forgiveness could be imparted. However, not all

24 *JJW*, vii, p. 275.
25 Ibid., vii, p. 273.
26 Ibid., vii, p. 297.
27 *JDJW*, iv, p. 268.
28 Ibid., v, p. 377–78.

prison visits were routine and one in particular, during his 1760 tour in Dublin, became a springboard for excursions into the wider field of public affairs. Prisoners taken in the Seven Years War became a source of concern for Wesley. In 1759 on a visit to Bristol he demonstrated sympathy for the plight of French prisoners of war held at Knowle. This led to further developments in Ireland. Some eighty-four French sailors captured after their raid on Carrickfergus in February 1760 were transported to Dublin. Wesley, made his way to minister to the captives. But he had an additional task in mind as become clear in a letter written some days later at Newry to Blackwell.[29] He informs him that he will shortly be at Carrickfergus and it is his intention to report on the campaign because he believes it to be of importance to the whole kingdom. Over the next days, in addition to his normal activities, he gathered information by speaking to people whose opinion he values, and interviewing French officers at both Carrickfergus and Moira. In the end he produced an account which is somewhat unique in that it to some extent reproduces the French point of view. More than that, however it demonstrated Wesley's growing confidence as a commentator on matters of general public concern. As his constant travels brought him up and down the land and across the channel (he usually stayed in London during the winter and began his travels each spring) he became an increasingly familiar figure throughout the kingdom. It was, for example, his own, as he saw it, almost unique experience and contact with ordinary people 'of the Americans on the one hand, or the English, Irish, or Scots on the other', which he used as a justification for writing some years later to Lord North on 'things that lie outside my province'—the affairs of America.[30]

It is in this light that his occasional addresses can best be understood and it was for similar reasons that he issued his *Compassionate Address to the Inhabitants of Ireland* in 1788. It was written to allay the fears of Irishmen who believed that their unprotected coast lay open to invasion from French and American privateers. 'I would fain speak a word of comfort to my poor neighbours, that they may not be frightened to death'. He enumerated the fears he had encountered throughout his travels on both sides of the channel, but which in Ireland had the additional threat of the enemy within, and then proceeded to dismiss them. His authority for so writing was that he felt he knew from his travels and contacts better than most what was really happening. His 'address' and the fears he seeks to allay reflects a more widespread and general insecurity than is suggested by an examination of letters and papers from official sources in a recent study on Francophobia in later eighteenth-century Irish history.[31]

29 J. Telford (ed.), *Letters of John Wesley* [hereafter *Letters*] (8 vols, London, 1844), iv, p. 94.
30 Ibid., vi, p. 161.
31 G. O'Brien, 'Francophobia in later eighteenth-century Irish History' in H. Gough & D. Dickson (eds) *Ireland and the French Revolution* (Dublin, 1990).

IV

The first issue to confront Wesley in Ireland was religious liberty which was a result of severe anti-Methodist rioting in Dublin, but particularly in Cork. Part of his response to that challenge was his *Letter to a Roman Catholic* which has received much recent attention. Apart from one reprint in 1825 it was not published again until the 1960s and matched an age of ecumenical discovery which followed the immediate post Vatican II period.[32] For all whose introduction to Wesley was by way of that letter it is something of a surprise to discover that his name came to be execrated in Catholic circles in his own lifetime, because of his opposition to the introduction of Saville's Relief Act in 1778. The action which precipitated the storm was a letter he wrote in 1780 to the *Public Advertiser* lending support for the Protestant Association's effort to have the act repealed. The propaganda war which flowed from it and the related Gordon riots determined Wesley's reputation, as well as the Methodists, among Catholics into the twentieth century. The immediate result of the controversy was that for the first time since his first visit in 1747 Wesley was advised for reasons of personal safety not to visit Ireland that year and indeed what had become bi-annual visits were interrupted by a gap of five years. He noted in his journal that many were grieved and offended by his letter and adds with less conviction than normal, 'I cannot help it. I must follow my own conscience'.[33] At the very least his timing was unfortunate. Even Charles Crookshank, who wrote his uniformly laudatory nineteenth century account of Wesley's life and times in Ireland, ventured the opinion that 'it would have been better had he not published just then, and in connection with the Protestant Association'.[34] The issues and chronology of the debate have been well covered[35] but the most serious long term effect was that the Methodists in these islands followed Wesley's lead in their attitude to the Catholic church.[36]

The attention given to Wesley's *Letter to a Roman Catholic* has tended to overshadow the fact that he issued two letters in 1749 within ten days of each other. The first addressed to *The Inhabitants of Ireland* [37] almost certainly had a Protestant constituency in view. Wesley, the Methodist leader, attempted to remove misunderstandings and explain the aims of his movement to those of

---

32 A well annotated edition was produced by a leading Irish Jesuit. Michael Hurley (ed.), *John Wesley's letter to a Roman catholic*, (London, 1968).
33 *JDJW*, vi, p. 159.
34 C.H. Crookshank, *History of Methodism in Ireland* (3 vols, London, 1885–8), i, p. 339.
35 D. Hempton, *Methodism and politics* (London, 1984); D. Butler, *Methodists and papists, John Wesley and the Catholic church in the eighteenth century* (London, 1995).
36 M. Edwards, *John Wesley and the eighteenth century* (London, 1933) p. 106; Hempton, *Methodism and politics*, p. 37.
37 J. Wesley, *A short address to the inhabitants of Ireland, occasioned by some late occurrences* (Dublin, 1749).

the established Anglican church. (To the end of his days he maintained he remained a faithful Church of England priest and that his religious societies were simply a renewal movement within that church.) In his *Letter to a Roman Catholic* Wesley did not specifically refer to Methodists but wrote as a priest of the Anglican church outlining those areas of Christian belief that both Protestants and Catholics hold in common and ended with a plea for mutual respect and the practice of the religion of love. These two letters written at the beginning of his Irish ministry reflected an underlying tension between the Anglican Wesley's insistence that his Methodist societies remain within the Church and the pragmatic religious leader anxious to respond to the spiritual needs of a wider constituency than those in the established church.

The model of Methodism as a reform movement intended to invigorate and operate within the structures of the established church made sense in England even if that was not how it worked in practice. But it was hopelessly inadequate in the very different religious situation into which it was imported in Ireland. Wesley's life long battle to prevent his movement from falling into dissent is sharper in Ireland than anywhere else. In correspondence with his preachers and at his Irish conferences he found the tension coming from at least four quarters. There were those who joined the Methodist movement who were Catholics, such as Thomas Walsh, perhaps the best Irish preacher he ever had, and who argued passionately for Independency in order to appeal to Catholics. Anglican clergy, such as Edward Smyth, who left the church in order to became itinerant preachers as a result of their evangelical zeal. Many of this type wished to break from the church they had left. Then there were those from a dissenting background particularly in Northern Ireland who never had any allegiance to the established church and could not understand why they should look to the Anglicans for their sacraments. Finally, there were those who because of their Methodist leanings had been persecuted or abused by clergy of the established church and found it difficult in their conscience to receive the sacraments from their hands. By sheer dint of personality Wesley managed to hold the societies in line and avoid secession from the church, but it was an exercise which required some degree of self-deception.

One of Wesley's itinerants Thomas Carlill was appointed to Lisburn in 1780. He was deeply unhappy and applied almost immediately to be allowed to return to England. His problem as he explained in a letter to Charles Wesley was that his congregations in Ireland were made up of Roman Catholics, Presbyterians, 'Seceders' and a few Anglicans. His difficulty was that his preaching appealed more to Anglican listeners 'so that I am quite out of my latitude in preaching to dissenters'.[38]

---

38 John Ryland's University Library of Manchester, DDPr 2/9, Catalogue of the early preachers collection, Thomas Carlil[l] to Charles Wesley, Bishop's Court, Ireland, 8 November 1780.

Carlill's problem was that he was the very model of a Methodist preacher, but he lacked the ability to adapt to a society where the rules did not really work. Wesley was without doubt the most adaptable and inventive religious leader of his age but he developed his plan of campaign in England and we can only begin to imagine what might have been had he been able, as he wished, to devote more of his time and energies to a land he undoubtedly loved but did not always understand.

Presbyterian Propaganda

RAYMOND GILLESPIE

The importance of the document printed here lies as much in its form as in its content. Those who have tried to chart the political activities of dissenters have concentrated on the lobbying of parliament or the discussion of political positions by clergy or ecclesiastical institutions. This document is directed at a wider audience and tries to explain the dissenting theological and political position in a form which was readily understood. This seems clear from two considerations. First, the document is printed in the form of a sixteen page pamphlet of which three copies survive, one in the British Library and two in the Bradshaw collection in Cambridge University Library.[1] Hence the text seems to have been intended for widespread distribution. Secondly, the versified form of the text would suggest that it was not simply intended for private reading but perhaps for public reading or, more likely, to make it easy for the illiterate to remember the arguments contained in it. As Roger Boyle, earl of Orrery, observed in 1681 there were those in Ireland who could scarcely repeat a sentence of scripture yet could recite entire psalms and rhymes since things were more easily learnt in verse.[2] From a dissenting perspective also learning large quantities of verse by rote seems to have been normal and the Dublin Presbyterian minister Joseph Boyse envisaged that hymns at family worship should be 'sung without reading' suggesting that these be memorised.[3] There is certainly a good deal of evidence that verse material was used by a range of groups in seventeenth-century Ireland. John Stearne, for instance, issued forty verse mediations for use during Lent 1691 and a religious autobiography by the Kilkenny Baptist Anne Fowkes is littered with stanza from religious poetry and hymns.[4] At a more political level verse also played a part. Shortly after the execution of John Atherton, the bishop

---

1 British Library, 11631 e 46; C.E. Sayle (ed.), *A catalogue of the Bradshaw collection of Irish books in the university of Cambridge* (3 vols, Cambridge, 1916), i, p. 280.
2 Roger Boyle, earl of Orrery, *Poems on most of the festivals of the church* (London, 1681), sig B1v.
3 Joseph Boyse, *Family hymns for morning and evening worship* (Dublin, 1701), sig A4.
4 J[ohn] S[tearne], *Seasonable thoughts in passion week* (Dublin, 1691); [Ann Fowkes], *A memoir of Mistress Ann Fowkes nee Geale* (Dublin, 1892).

of Waterford convicted of sodomy in 1640, some 'scandalous rhyming pamphlets' were circulating and when the death of the prominent Jacobite Henry Luttrell was rumoured in 1717 the Dublin Tory printer Cornelius Carter seeing a market commissioned a verse elegy for sale as a broadsheet.[5] The text below would seem to fit into this tradition of the printing of verse texts to popularise religious or political positions.

This context raises questions of the date and authorship of the text. While the text itself is not dated a range of dates are suggested by the printer's name and address. The business of the printer, John Afleck, collapsed in 1721 which provides *terminus a quem* for the text. The poem cannot have been composed earlier than 1716 when he moved to the address in the imprint.[6] Moreover, the last speech by the meeting house suggests that some concessions had been made to the dissenting cause which is almost certainly a reference to the Toleration Act of November 1719. This final speech is rather out of character with the rest of the text which is more defensive in tone and it may have been added at the last moment. Thus the text may have been written in early 1719 while the campaign for toleration was being waged and published in late 1719 after it was granted.[7]

Just as the text is not dated neither is there any author given. This was not unusual in controversial works and at least some of the popular political verses issued in early eighteenth-century Dublin were written by hacks or in one case schoolboys.[8] In this case, however, this seems unlikely given the familiarity of the author with the complexities of the religious and political positions of both dissenters and the established church. It seems likely that the author had some familiarity with the controversies between these groups over the previous thirty years. The text is written from a dissenting perspective. It is the meeting house, for example, which has the final triumphant word celebrating the limiting of the power of the Church of Ireland. The figure who best fits these criteria is the Dublin Presbyterian minister Joseph Boyse who was minister of the Wood Street congregation, which stood near St Patrick's cathedral. Moreover, Boyse had an interest in versification, compiling two collections of hymns for use in Dublin and his son Samuel became a poet in his own right.[9] The issues which are reflected in the verses, such as the forms of worship and church government, are

5   Nicholas Bernard, *The penitent death of a woeful sinner* (Dublin, 1641), 'To the reader'; J.T. Gilbert, *History of the city of Dublin* (3 vols, Dublin, 1854-9), i, pp 63-5. Verses for the arrival of the lord lieutenant were also printed in 1677, Marquis of Lansdowne (ed.), *The Petty-Southwell correspondence, 1676-87* (London, 1928), p. 33.
6   Robert Munter, *A dictionary of the print trade in Ireland, 1550-1775* (New York, 1988), p. 14.
7   For the campaign J.C. Beckett, *Protestant dissent in Ireland, 1687-1780* (London, 1948), pp. 71-82, and David Hayton's essay above.
8   Gilbert, *History of the city of Dublin*, i, p. 64.
9   Joseph Boyse, *Sacramental hymns* (Dublin, 1693); Boyse, *Family hymns*. For Samuel Boyse see *Dictionary of National biography*, sub nomine.

those which Boyse had debated in print with William King, bishop of Derry, in the 1690s.[10]

The document printed below therefore seems to represent an attempt by a dissenting controversialist to translate arguments between churchmen into a popular form in the context of political agitation for toleration. It thus provides a glimpse of the popular politics of dissent in early eighteenth-century Ireland. The text is printed in the original and has not been modernised with the exception of the correction of a few obvious typographical errors.

10 For an overview, Phil Kilroy, *Protestant dissent and controversy in Ireland, 1660–1714* (Cork, 1994), pp. 171–87.

Ecclesia & reformatio
OR, A
DIALOGUE
BETWEEN
St. Patrick's Church
and
Wood-Street Meeting-House.

In Nova fert Animus,
Mutatas dicere formas,
Corpora.
Ovid[11]

DUBLIN
Printed for John Afleck Bookseller at
Buchanan's Head in *Dames-Street.*

---

11 'My mind is bent to tell of bodies changed into new forms', Ovid, *Metamorphoses*,
book i, line 1.

[p.2] [blank]

[p.3]   Meeting-House.

Tell Me great Fabrick! tho' Our Distance seems,
Something Remote,[12] why should our Converse cease.
Altho' they Spire attempts the distant Skies,
And thy high Roof does o're our Houses rise,
Altho thy Pomp and Gilded Altar shine,
By Holy Sanction and a Right Divine,
Submisive People tremble at it's Nod,
And Worship it, tho' they profane their God,
Yet suffer me that I enquire the Cause,
Why thus thou'rt raised and by what mighty Laws,
Some are by force unto thy Altars brought,
Compelled to bow or Impiously you break,
What your Faith calls the Stiff and Stubborn Neck,
[p.4] You're strength is like some *Whale* upon the Sea,
That makes the trembling Fishes to obey,
Or else you execute pretended Power,
The Right Divine is given you to Devour.

              St. Patricks.

The Power I represent excessive in your thought,   )
By Holy Writ we're taught,   )
From confus'd Atoms was to Order brought:)
The Days and Years in regular State began,
And ever since in just Procession ran.
Nature exhorbitant does often grow,
And Blood flows sometime high, ebbs often low:
But in Religion a Decorum's us'd,
Its Rights are orderly and not confus'd,
The brainless Mob wild Passions do controul,
And Infant-Saints need Guardians to the Soul;
Spiritual Doctors don't the Patient please,
But sute the Medicines to the great Disease:
If grown delerious, Physick is refus'd,
Force for the Patient's good, must then be us'd.

              Meeting-House.

If human Laws may force a human Mind,
One's fancy may another's Conscience bind,

---

12 Since the meeting house is Wood Street, whichwas near St Patrick's, this statement should
be taken as a comment on the theological position of the disputants rather than a measure of physical distance.

And those who never own'd a God at all,
At least do blindly serve and bow to *Baal*.[13]
Make Terms of their Communion wrong or right,
If all Religion must be made by Might;
We chuse a Doctor for our Body's Health,
And give him Fees according to our Wealth:
[p.5] We try his Med'cines, then approve his Skill,
But think no Law impowers him to kill:
The Heav'nly Quacks no Power can controul,
They have a Right Divine to kill the Soul:
Spiritual Physick we must take by force;
You drench the Soul, as Farriers do a Horse.
Where Doctors thus Man's Reason do invade,
The Patient's sober, and the Doctor's mad:
Had not the Mortal must such Toils endure,
Better be damn'd than undergo the Cure:
For where the Church such Recipes does bring,
Saving and Damning is the self same thing.
The Laws in Faith can no Direction give;
By Grace Divine and Reason we believe:
Thou' we our Hopes in Reason do not place,
Yet Reason follows, or is join'd with Grace.
The Spirit's Work no humane Law controuls,
And Reason tells th' effect it has on Souls.
In vain the Soul with humane Laws you bind,
In senseless Shackles fetter up the Mind,
Which like th' eternal Thought is unconfin'd:
As if our Sense was only fit for Trade,
And Reason never for Religion made:
And must not of our Souls concern debate,
But blindly grope for an eternal State.
       St. Patricks.
Reason may be on humbling Surges tost,
Or, not well govern'd in the Clouds, be lost:
Reason in all things ought to have its due,
But still have proof to know that *Reason*'s true.
[p.6] 'This plain how often Men do change their Mind;
Oft as the Tides, or the unconstant Wind;
Continual Errors 'mongst the wise abound,

13 Baal is the standard Old Testament description of a pagan diety, for example 1 Kings
    18:22–30, 2 Kings 10:18–23, Jeremiah 11:13–17.

And not one Man infallible is found:
How oft the *Judgment* leads the Man aside;
And *Reason* wanders when it has no Guide.
I mark the way your *Reason* ought to go,
And the best Path to Heav'nly Mansions show;
By me directed you may overcome
The crooked Serpent,[14] and the Whore of *Rome*;[15]
I am founded upon the *Rock* Divine,[16]
I am your Guide, and the blest Scripture's mine.
The Holy Word, my *Charter* and Delight,
And National States have recogniz'd my Right.
If stubborn Souls my Precepts cannot draw,
I must convert 'em by the force of Law.
The Body's Pleasure did the Soul oppress,
Made Mankind fall into Unhappiness.
The Body justly its Afflictions hath,
To save the Soul from an eternal Wrath.
Think it not hard if I Chastiment give,
I scourge the Flesh, to make the Consciense live
　　　　　　　　Meeting-House.
I know our *Reason* may be in the dark,
And blunder oft, and often miss the mark;
But the *All-wise* his Councils can unfold,
And give his *Spirit* as he did of old.
The mighty Truths of th' Eternal Word
No aids of humane *Reason* can afford:
The Light Divine is evermore conceal'd,
But by the *God of Light* himself reveal'd,
[p.7] Whose *Spirit* reaches to the inward Parts,
He views the secret corners of our Hearts:[17]
Where you my *Guide*, I needs must go astray.
When only *Jus Divinum* leads the way:
How can you me a safe Instruction grant,
Who know not half the Mercies I do want?
What Stings of Conscience I within me feel,

14　The reference is to Satan or the Devil, Genesis 3:1, II Corinthinians 11:3, Revelation 12:9.
15　The Papacy.
16　Ascription given in the Bible to God in the Old Testament, e.g. Psalm 19:14, 31:3, and Christ in the New Testament, e.g. Romans 9:33.
17　These verses are referring to the work of the Holy Spirit in guiding the faithful, Romans 8:27; I Corinthians 2:10 ff.

Or Apprehensions of approaching Hell;
A Guide to *Reason* of a nobler Make
Than what of humane Fraility does partake.
How can your *Reason* be a Guide to mine,
When both our *Reason's* equally divine;
Thro equal Clouds and daily Errors pass,
And differ only as improv'd by *Grace*.
The *Scripture* only is our Reason's Guide,
And all is Noise and Foolishness beside.
Lay by the *Law* and thy Foundation's gone,
Thou art not built upon the Corner-stone.[18]
By Humane Power thou art wonderous great,
But Civil Sanction proves a Human Cheat;
The Church of *Christ* to endless Ages blest,
Can of itself, without a Law, subsist.
When Foes invade her, she has no Recourse
To weak Auxiliries of humane Force.
Our blessed *Saviour* has no Pow'r given
To mortal man the change to Laws of Heav'n.
Th' eternal Law do's ev'ry where suffice
To rule the Church, and to instruct the Wise.
If you to mend it do a Power own,
By the same Power you may pull it down:
'Tis highest Arrogance to think that you
In making *Forms* our Saviour can out do[19].
[p.8] If only *Law* thy boasted *Basis* be;
The *Pagan* Temples are as good as thee;
The Law, that thy Prayers does impose on Man,
Imposes also the *Turks Alcoran*.[20]
When back'd with Pow'r your *Articles* you give,
We do at best implicity believe.

18 Corner-stone is a reference to Christ, Matthew 21:42, Luke 20:17, Ephesians 2:20, I Peter 2:7.
19 The discussion here moves into forms of worship, the author objecting to set forms of worship such as the Prayer Book. This had been a central point in the 1690s debate between Boyse and King, Boyse taking the position that 'where God has enjoined any part of religious worship in general but has not determined the particular mode and circumstances of it there the determination belongs to human prudence' and hence there were no divine forms apart from those specifically enjoined in scripture such as the Lords Prayer, Joseph Boyse, *Remarks on a late discourse of William, lord bishop of Derry* (London, 1694), pp. 9, 40.
20 Koran.

St. Patricks.

I do not the eternal Law infringe,
Nor do the Churches Constitution change;
My Laws were never necessary meant,
But left to Souls as things indifferent:
The *Modes* of Worship are no part of *Faith,*
I do believe but what the *Scripture* saith.
But by the Power above 'tis left to me
T'appoint what *Modes* there shall in Worship be.
My Rites are all conform unto the Word,
And heav'nly Comfort to the Soul afford:
I in my *Choice* transporting Raptures find,
Seraphick Strains, and an exalted Mind.
These are the Blessings I impose on you,
For which, Apostate, I am deem'd your foe.

Meeting-House.

By things Indifferent I am betray'd;
For still I find 'em necessary made:
My Sons by these have often been undon
Their Souls beneath thy gilded *Altars* groan;[21]
Stifl'd in *Prisons*, robb'd of Liberty,[22]
For Non-compliance to thy Foppery:
Which (tho to Forms Divine thou mak'st pretence)
Have no alliance unto common Sense.
[p.9] Thy mimick Postures, and thy senseless Bows,
Thy gilded Organs, and Theatrick Rows
Of Fidlers, Harpers, Singing-men, an[d] Boys,
Praising of God in a confounded noise;
Can bawdy Ballads chant, or sacred Hymn,
One day a *Fiddler*, next a *Seraphim*:
He whose polluted Breath but t'other day,
Charmed the lew'd Audience at a bawdy Play,
Sings with the same lewd Breath within thy *Quire,*
And tunes his Voice to *David's* sacred *Lyre*.
I peep'd within thy Gates the other day;
(For Novelty may lead the best astray)
I view'd thy Altar, and the gilded Wood;
Where in the Corner a strange *Songster* stood;

21 This is a reference to martyrs wanting to be avenged, Revelation 6:9,10.
22 The Act of Uniformity of 1666 provided for penalties for those dissenters failing to attend services of the established church. These were removed by the Toleration Act of 1719 which suggests this part of he text may preceed that act.

A *Goldfinch* he appear'd unto the Sight,
His sacred Vestments were of red and white
But when he open'd his unhallow'd Throat,
He seemed some croaking *Raven* by his Note:
Prodigious Scare-crow on his perch was rear'd,
To warn the old, and make the young afraid;
Lord how with gogle Eyes he wonders at
Some mighty something is the Lord knows what;
Extends his Arms, as Angels do their Wings,
Seems to mount upward, as below he sings.
This, this the Worship, which thy Laws ordain;
Thus, thus the Sacred Name is took in vain:
Thus Men their reason and their Sense confound,
And chuse Religion by an empty Sound
Me Sounds alike do please; the croaking Frogs
Thy Nest of Whistles: or the Drove of Hogs.
I teach my Sons Humility and Love,
And all the Graces furnish'd from Above;
Not frothy Notions, Philosophick Pride,
But Christ for ruin'd Sinners crucify'd;
[p. 10] How they unruly Passions should subdue,
Discharge the Old man, and recieve the New;[23]
I bid 'em still for Sufferings preprare,
And be provided for the Christian War,
Gainst days of Persecution shall return,
And they, as Saints of old, for Faith may burn:
I bid 'em oft in Mediatations be,
And tho thou ha'st my Children, pray for thee.
                    St. Patricks.
My Sacred Rites have bin approv'd by all,
We Orthodox and holy Fathers call,
And learned Prelates above all the rest,
Lately deceas'd, and numbered with the Blest,
Whose holy Lives have demonstration giv'n,
They were the Darlings of the Church and Heav'n,
'Tis want of Knowledge makes you thus dissent:
You should, you should your Ignorance lament;
Your Native Sowrness and Stupidity,
Two ill Companions for a Christian be:
While you no harmles Ceremonies grant,

---

23 This refers to Paul's admonitions in Ephesians 4:22–24 and Colossians 3:9,10.

You break the Windows to destroy the Paint;
Because you find irregular the Porch,
You are resolv'd to batter down the Church.
Thus some craz'd Marriner upon the Deep,
To drown the Rats, does madly sink his Ship.
You can no good by my Devotion feel,
Nor will before my sacred Alters kneel,
But for Preferment, or a wealthy Place,
Interest usurps, and baffles conquer'd Grace;
Your Sons assemble, and with mine recieve
The Sacrament, as I the same do give;
Nought of their former Faith do's then remain,
They ride the Horse, but Interest guides the Rein.[24]
[p. 11]   Meeting-House.
On Fathers, Councils, Synods, or Decrees,
I don't rely, or guide my Faith by these.
Of human Race all our Fore-fathers were,
Oft left the Good, and with the Bad did err:
When ere their Doctrins do a Doubt afford,
I bring it to the Touchstone of the Word.
I ne'er cou'd think the righteous God would give
Power to one, for others to believe,
Or that a Father had a right to be
Judg for himself and his Posterity.
My Sons thou slander'st, and call'st ignorant,
Thy Sons, tho learn'd, do all the Graces want:
My Sons too could their human Learning boast,
But that in things and of God and Faith is lost,
Can'st thou the Spirit, and the Fathers Love,
By Mathamatick Demonstration prove,
Why God Religion in this Land should place,
And to so many Lands deny his Grace?
In human Learning we no Profit find,
For human things affect a human Mind;
The things of God a nobler heat require   )
Our Souls are touch'd with a Celestial Fire,   )
Which tho we can't concieve, we must admire.   )
The blessed Martyrs in the days of old
My sacred Truths and Doctrins sound did hold;

24 This refers to the Sacramental test for public office introduced in 1704, Kilroy, *Protestant dissent*, pp 188–93..

Did the same Faith, and the same Worship teach,
Alike they worship'd, and alike did preach:
Their Learning was their Persecutors shame;
But 'twas God's Spirit led'm through the Flame.
Nature oppress'd by Nature, quits the Field,
Without divine assistance soon do's yield:
[p. 12] My Sons to many, and alas too weak,
Do at thy altars their Preferments seek:
Where Int'rest rules, the weaker Graces fall,
And men corrupted bow the Knee to *Baal*,
Side with the World for Profit and Estate,
But these my Sons are illegitimate;[25]
Creep to my Altars 'mongst the numerous Thron
Not well instructed to continue long:
But if God's Word, and Sacrament divine,
Be thus abus'd, the fault is wholly thine:
I blame my Sons who with thy Laws do close,
But more I blame thee dost those Laws impose;
Laws which the Rights of Nature do infringe,
Corrupt the Faith and Ordinances change;
Thus alter'd, thus directed, are at best
Only a secular and human Test:
To ruin Faith you Votaries decoy,
For thus to alter's wholly to destroy.
While you in Pow'r your vast Dominion place,   )
you do the worth of sacraments debase,   )
The ill effects of a corrupted Grace.   )
Thy Sons by Prophets are grown wonderous great;
Why are my Sons excluded from the State?
Thy Sons grow proud, while mine you thus debar;
For Pride and Power still consistent are:
My Sons are all excluded from the Court,
And must not serve a *Monarch* they support;
A *King* they love, a *Settlement* they own,
And did their best to bring him to the *Throne*;
For him they always most devoutly *pray*,
That Heav'n would bless, and still direct his way:
I teach my Infants his just Praise to sing,   )
For him my Lute and trembling Harp I string,   )

25 Hebrews 12:8.

And all my Sons are loyal to the *King*.[26]   )
[p. 13] Thy Sons are disobedient to the Laws,
And traiterously embark in a bad Cause,
Would all our Rights and Liberties betray,
Set up the Slave, and take the Man away:
Some of thy Sons ingloriously contriv'd:
To take that Life away by which they liv'd;
With murderous Hands that Sacred King to seize,
Which sav'd our sinking Nations in distress.
Their villanous Acts and their detested Fame
Our City Gates do all around proclaim.
                    St. Patricks.
How ill pronounc'd is sacred Loyaltie,
By thy inhuman, murderous Brood and Thee?
What mighty Mischiefs heretofore you've don,
Murder'd the Father, and depos'd the Son;[27]
You loyal prove only to gain by Stealth
That hideous ill shap'd thing, a Commonwealth,
Which better with your Discipline might sute,
More rigid far than mine, and absolute:
My Sons were never from Rebellion free,
Much fam'd for their unspotted Loyalty.
I the best Guardian to a Monarch's Throne,
All my rebellious Children do disown:
Thy Sons uneasy do promote our Wars,
Bred up to Factions, and intestine Jars;
Ill natur'd, insolent, corupt and bad,
Morose, perverse, and mischievously mad,
Turbulent, proud, impatient in distress,
Their Sins to God nor Man they will confess;
Sprung from the Loins of Angels as they fell,[28]
Averse to Good, and easy to rebel;
Bold Mariners who 'mongst the Rocks do steer,
Always rejoycing when a Storm is near;
[p. 14] On swelling Seas the most contentment find,
Pleas'd with the Noise and Russling of the Wind:

---

26 Presbyterian loyalty to the Glorious Revolution was one of the key stones of the arguments of Boyse and others for toleration and was most forcefully advanced by James
  Kirkpatrick, *An historical essay upon the loyalty of presbyterians* ([Belfast], 1713).
27 This refers to the execution of Charles I and the overthrow of his son James II.
28 This refers to the story of angels breeding with human women found in Genesis 6:1–8

Bout 'feu's that always light Dissention's Torch,
Loading with Pasquils still the harmless Church.
Meeting-House
My Sons are gentle, and avoid Disputes,
Contention ill with their kind temper sutes:
Not haughty, puff'd, nor insolently proud,
Stoops to Superiors humble to the Crowd:
Reverence the Good, nor do the Bad despise,   )
Pitty the Fools, and do applaud the Wise,   )
And Kindness show ev'n to their Enemies:)
Yet never think the Laws of God provide
The Saint should lay the Englishman aside.
The Laws of Nature, and of common sense
Allow all Men to speak in their Defence.
If thy Sons rudely will my Children use,
Of Crimes unknown thus falsely will accuse,
Their native Innocence they then must clear,   )
Asses and Camels must hard Burdens bear;   )
To Men of worth their Reputation's dear,   )
'Gainst them industriously thine always toil,
The very Dragons of thy Church revile;
And each dull Weathercock thou moun'st aloft
Has both at me and at my Children scoft:
Thy Dragon does declare thy Infants Breed,
That all thy Sons are of the Serpents Seed;
The Church that's represented by a Dragon,
Proves that its Head and chief support is *Dagon*:[29]
Which lately has within a neighbring Land
Stumbl'd before the Ark, and lost his Hand.
Each wretched Mortal such a Fate will find,
Who is averse to the Eternal Mind.
[p. 15] Thy *Babel* Spire,[30] as it do upwards rise,
May feel the Fury of the angry Skies:
And thy old Towers now are grown so tall,
May by loud Thunder and fork'd Lightening fall.
Thou sayest my Sons are a rebellious Brood,
And have their hands in Blood of Kings imbrew'd:
My Sons did ne'r molest a righteous State,
But Tyranny they always grumbl'd at:

29 Judges, 16: 23, I Samuel, 5: 1–8.
30 Refers to the tower of Babel, Genesis 11:1–9.

'Tis not their fault if Kings do Tyrants grow,
Prove their own Ruin and their Overthrow:
They may their Actions and their Crimes condemn,
But 'tis just Heav'n alone does punish them.
St. Patricks.
Thus for my Kindness I'm rewarded still,
My Goodness thus excites you unto ill:
Thy senseless Schism I always do lament,
And dread thy Danger, which I would prevent:
But good Advice and Arguments are in vain,
To Men perplex'd with a distracted Brain.
I would have drawn thee with Cords of Love,   )
The gentle Method of my Head above,   )
But all my means do unsuccessful prove.   )
When these kind Methods I have laid aside,
I, what Correction can affect, have try'd:
But neither Love nor Wrath was understood,
Doom'd to be stubborn, and estrang'd to good!
I all my Ends and good Intentions mist,
Whilst thou in thy Perversness didst persist:
The most unweildy, resty thing alive,
A wayward Beast will neither lead nor drive:
But yet to thee I open still my Gate,
Hadst thou but Grace to enter in thereat.
[p. 16] Beneath my Roof I have preserv'd a Room
For thee and all thy Sons that thither come;
Where a safe Shelter thou mayest always find
From wasting Rains, and the tempestous Wind.
Meeting-House
Thus some great Lion of the *Lybian* Brood,
Who long has reign'd and ravag'd all the Wood,
The harmless Herds his rav'nous Paws has kill'd,
Whose murder'd Carkasses his Gets have fill'd:
Grown old he can't so nimbly frisk about,
Or if he's muzzl'd, or his Teeth beat out,
Contracts his Paws, seems lovingly inclin'd,
Feeds with the Does, and slumbers with the Hind.[31]
'Tho now he can't, as once, so loudly roar,
Nor be as cruel as he was before;

---

31 The allusion here is probably to John Dryden's 'The hind and panther' (1687) in
which the Catholic church is depicted as the 'mile-white Hind'.

His Mind's the same, and always bent to ill;
Nature unchang'd, he is a Lion still.
How kindly now my Sons you do invite,
Who know you're muzzl'd, and you cannot bite:
My Sons supported by the self same Law,
Which once expos'd them to the Lions Paw:
Nor need they now to thee for Shelter come,
Since Law secures them in their Faith at home:
Beneath thy Shade no generous Plant will grow,
Thy Shade's destructive as the Frost or Snow.
The Beasts which o're the flowry Pastures range
May for thy Shadow sultry Beams exchange,
But soon return to Herbage in the Field;
Thy Shelter does no wholesom Pasture yield.

FINIS

Index